Website Management

Geoff Elliott

Lexden Publishing
www.lexden-publishing.co.uk

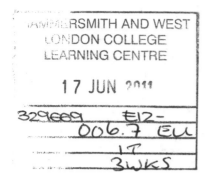
First published in 2007 by Lexden Publishing Ltd.

British Library Cataloguing in Publication Data
A CIP record for this book is available from the British Library.

ISBN: 978 1 904995 21 0

Printed by Lightning Source

Lexden Publishing Ltd
23 Irvine Road
Colchester
Essex
C03 3TS

Tel: 01206 533164
Email: **info@lexden-publishing.co.uk**
www.lexden-publishing.co.uk

CONTENTS

Chapter 1

INTRODUCTION

Chapter overview

This chapter outlines for whom this book is intended, how to use it and provides some useful study skill tips. This followed by an outline of what website management is and how each chapter addresses its various aspects.

Learning outcomes

Having read this chapter you should:

- know how to use the book;
- apply key study skills techniques to help you study website management;
- define website management.

1.1: Introduction

This book is aimed at a range of different types of reader and is suited to students studying at:

- level 3 (e.g. A levels IT, NVQ level 3);
- level 4 and 5 (e.g. HND, Foundation degree);
- level 6 (e.g. second year of a degree programme);

The typical courses for which this book would be useful include:

- Degrees, HNDs or HNCs courses in:
  - computing;
  - Internet technologies;
  - information technology;
  - web design;
  - web development;
  - multimedia computing;
  - web technologies;
  - A level Applied ICT;

- Advanced GCE in Applied ICT;
- NVQ level 3 in:

    - business and administration;

    - IT professionals;

    - data management for web design;

    - ICT;

- ITQ level 3 (module intranets and Internets);
- British Computing Society Diploma in IT;
- BTEC National Diploma IT for Practitioners.

The book is also useful to anyone who has a website or intranet, but wishes to know more about how to develop, manage and market it.

Assumptions

This book assumes readers will already have some experience of building web pages and will understand the basics of the technologies behind the Internet and the web. Ideally, readers should have experience of building web pages with a basic HTML editor as well as using web development tools, for example Microsoft FrontPage or Adobe Dreamweaver[1].

1.2: How to use this book

When you read this book or any text book you should ask yourself "**why** am I reading it?" because this will influence how you tackle it. Try following these tips:

Set objectives – try to define what information you are looking for and what you wish to do with it.

Survey – skim through the whole book to get an overview of what it is about and how it is structured.

Think and link – how do the contents relate to what you already know and does it meet your objectives? Make notes or add to your existing notes, ensuring you record where in the book you found something – you might want to return to it.

---

1 Formerly owned by Macromedia

Each chapter of this book is structured along these lines:

Chapter overview	Outlines the purpose of the chapter
Learning outcomes	The learning outcomes for each chapter are listed. Having read the chapter and completed the end of chapter example questions, you should achieve the learning outcomes.
Assessment	How you are likely to be assessed on the content of a chapter.
Content sections	The body of each chapter is broken down into discrete sections.
Chapter Summary	A review of the subject matter covered by the chapter.
Example questions	A number of example questions testing the knowledge contained in the chapter.
Answers	Indicative answers to the example questions.
Further research and reading	Details of websites and books where readers can find out more.

You can read each chapter independently, but there is a significant number of cross references in the book from one section to another, so you might need to jump around a little. Any word or phrase that is highlighted is a key concept or principle that you need to ensure you fully understand.

When you begin to focus on the book in more detail, the best way to use it is to:

1. study the learning outcomes for each chapter carefully;

2. read the content of the chapter;

3. try answering the example questions at the end of the chapter (you only need to make a series of bullet points of how you would answer). You can refer to the contents of the chapter, but avoid looking at the answers;

4. check your answers against the ones given. Remember the given answers are not the only answers; and

5. refer back to the learning outcomes at the beginning of the chapter to check that you have achieved them.

The references at the end of the end of each chapter are usually websites rather than books since these are more immediately available to readers than books.

1.3: Study skills

There are many websites offering good advice on study skills including your own institution and some are listed at the end of this chapter. Here are some general tips on making notes, revising and completing assignments or examinations.

Making notes:

- focus on summarising in bullet points what you read in this book, don't quote word for word;

- use highlighter pens to mark key points; and

- use your own 'shorthand', such as '=' for 'equals', 'e.g.' for 'for example', '→' for 'causes' or 'leads to' or 'implies'.

Many people prefer visual notes or **rich pictures** to text-based notes, i.e. drawing rather than writing. *Figure 1.1* shows an example of a rich picture for note taking. Some people use **spider diagrams** or **mind maps** as shown in *Figure 1.2* where the subject of interest is written down in the middle of the page and all the elements of the subject are drawn as 'branches' coming off the central theme. A mind map can be embellished with colour and extra sketches to help recall later. Another technique is called **concept mapping** as shown in *Figure 1.3* where the main concepts are linked by directional arrows. It is fine, however, to mix text-based note-taking with visual notes, it is something only you will know which is best for you.

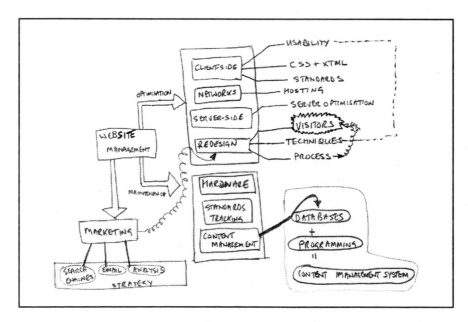

Figure 1.1: An example of a rich picture of the subject 'Website management'

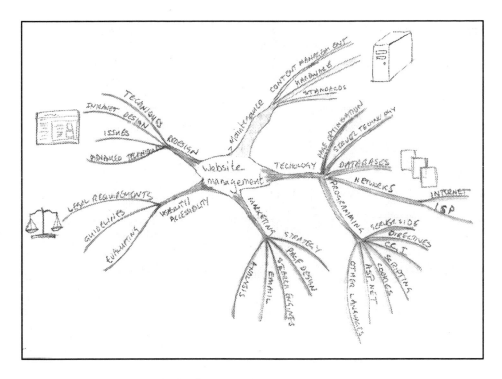

*Figure 1.2: An example of a spider diagram/rich picture of the subject
'Website management'*

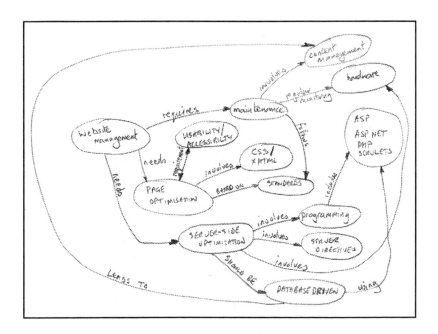

*Figure 1.3: Example of a concept map of the subject
'Website management'*

Visual note taking can be done with computer applications, such as Microsoft PowerPoint and there are specialist programs for mind mapping, for example Mind Genius (*see Further reading and research, page 11* for details).

Revision

It is not particularly effective just to read through notes over and over. The most effective ways to revise are those where you interact with the subject and making it meaningful to you, for example:

- give yourself a problem on the subject and then try to answer it;
- rework the material into a picture;
- try summarising material into fewer and fewer words or pictures;
- discuss the subject with other people; and
- make links, comparisons and contrasts between different areas of the subject.

If you are revising for an exam you should:

- start several weeks before the exam;
- make a revision timetable;
- answer questions from past papers;
- identify the key points plus an example and some evidence for each sub-topic;
- be prepared for questions that combine two different topics; and
- ensure that you go through each subject over and over rather than just revise each subject in detail just once.

1.4: What is website management?

Website management means many things, but for the purposes of this book we assume that there is a website already in existence and that it must be 'managed'. In this context, the management of a website means ensuring the site:

- meets its purpose (its purpose might have changed since its creation) efficiently and effectively;
- is based on the most appropriate and efficient technology;
- ensures visitors have an enjoyable/pleasurable experience;
- is as useable as is practical;
- runs as cost effectively as possible; and
- reaches its target audience as cost effectively as possible.

What these requirements mean is that every aspect of the site must be evaluated and then changes made when and where necessary. Some evaluations will be periodic and some constant, including:

- the technology used to build the web pages of the site – *Chapter 2, pages 13–34*;

- the back-end technologies used to deliver the site – *Chapter 3, pages 35–52, Chapter 4, pages 53–74* and *Chapter 5, pages 75–92* and *Chapter 6, pages 93–108*;

- the layout, structure and look and feel of the site – *Chapter 7, pages 109–124*;

- the content of the site – *Chapter 8, pages 125–138*;

- the marketing of the site – *Chapter 9, pages 139–156*; and

- the suitability of the site for its purpose – *Chapter 10, pages 157–168* and *Chapter 11, pages 169–180*.

A significant proportion of website management is ensuring the back-end technologies are right. This means the:

- web server software and hardware delivering the site;

- network configuration of the site, i.e. who hosts the site and what is their level of service, e.g. bandwidth;

- back-end programming environments used to build the site; and

- databases used to contain and maintain the content.

This is why four chapters of this book (*Chapters 3–6*) are dedicated to the back-end technology.

1.5:   The book's structure

2	Web page optimisation	You should have some experiencing of designing and building web pages. This chapter looks at the client-side technologies that can be used to optimise web pages in terms of speed of download and their ease of use.
3	Web servers	This chapter goes into the detail of what are web servers and how they work. Then it compares the two leading web server applications.
4	Network and connection considerations	This chapter looks at the underlying network issues of website management as well as the important issues of how you make your website available to others to see. It also looks at how you create intranets and extranets.
5	Web server programming	This chapter examines the various programming languages and environments used to create dynamic websites.
6	Databases and web servers	This chapter looks at the issues of how databases are integrated with web servers and how web forms are used to obtain data from users.
7	Website redesign	If you have had a website for a while, how do you go about redesigning it? This chapter also looks at the specific issues of the design of intranets.
8	Website maintenance	What are the principles and issues of maintaining a website? What should you be doing to maintain your website?
9	Website marketing	How do you get your website known and how do you keep people returning to your site? This chapter covers all the important techniques for website marketing.
10	E-commerce and other web-based applications	This chapter covers the most important of web applications – e-commerce as well as the other top applications.
11	Accessibility and usability	The key to getting people to return to your website is improving its accessibility to all people and making it as easy to use as possible. This chapter covers the main guidelines and tips as well as the current accessibility legislation.

Assessment

It is difficult to arrange practical assessment of website management because much of it requires an existing site and access to the back-end of a web server to which students can apply and test out the principles learnt. More likely is that students are expected to find an existing site on the web to which they can make recommendations on how the site should be managed and maintained. Students might also be expected to answer case study or hypothetical-type questions in examinations and asked to advise on how website management principles can be applied.

1.6:   Further reading and research

Books

Cunliffe, D and Elliott, G. (2005) *Multimedia Computing*, Lexden Publishing: Colchester.

Websites

Add the number in square brackets to **www.bookref.net/lpwm** for the most up to date web link, for example www.bookref.net/lpwm0110

http://openlearn.open.ac.uk – the Open University's free Moodle-based learning environment including free resources on study skills. [0101]

www.ltscotland.org.uk/studyskills/15to18/index.asp – study skill resources. [0102]

www.mindtools.com/pages/article/newISS_00.htm – more study skill resources. [0103]

Chapter 2

WEB PAGE OPTIMISATION

Chapter overview

In this chapter we will look at standards and methods that can be used to optimise the performance and accessibility of a web page including:

- Cascading Style Sheets (CSS);

- eXtensible Hypertext Mark-up Language (XHTML); and

- eXtensible Mark-up Language (XML).

Advice and guidance is given; however, detailed coverage of these standards is not provided and you are advised to look at the *Further reading and research on page 34.*

Learning outcomes

It is assumed that you would have already been designing and building web pages using an HTML editor or with authoring tools. After studying this chapter and answering the example questions at the end of the chapter, you should be able to achieve these outcomes:

Outcome 1: Apply W3C standards to web page design.

Outcome 2: Apply optimising techniques to improve the download speeds of web pages.

Outcome 3: Decide when to use XML in producing web pages and other documents.

How will you be assessed on this?

In earlier course work in previous modules, you would have created a basic website using HTML, probably using a web page authoring tool. You should be able to demonstrate an understanding of the appropriate use of advanced web page technologies and how to make a website standards-compliant. An examination question, might ask you to explain what are the various web standards and what technologies to use to create compliant web pages. You might be given a particular case study or scenario and asked to come up with the best approach to the development of the site.

2.1: Introduction

You should have had some experience of creating web pages in 'raw' **HTML (Hypertext Markup Language)** and also with authoring tools such as Adobe Dreamweaver or Microsoft FrontPage. There are many other technologies that can be used to create web pages, some are generated dynamically from server-based programs or scripts, some are generated dynamically in the browser (often referred to as **Dynamic HTML (DHTML)**) using scripting languages such as JavaScript and others use proprietary plugin technologies such as Adobe Flash. A single web page may be created using a combination of technologies, for example a page that is partially generated at the server-side, but also includes elements of JavaScript and Flash.

The problem with developing web pages is ensuring that your design will appear as you want it to in each of the different makes and versions of browser, screen resolutions and colour depths, operating systems and platforms (including mobile devices). Using a range of technologies to create and display your pages compounds this problem. The old adage:

Keep It Simple, Stupid – **KISS**

has a lot of merit when creating web pages, if you use only a limited set of web technologies, they are more likely to display correctly, whatever the arrangement of browser, operating system or platform the end-user has.

In addition to the 'KISS' principle is the **standards-compliant** principle. Ensuring that your pages are standards-compliant will improve the chances that your pages will display correctly, wherever and whatever they are displayed on. A web technology standard is an agreed specification of a mark-up or programming language that all the important organisations and companies world wide (software, hardware, telecom companies, universities) implement in a consistent way. The **World Wide Web Consortium (W3C)** produces the standards for web technologies and is explained in *Section 2.2, page 15.*

Another important principle is to ensure that you make the size of your web pages as small as possible so that they download quickly. This includes ensuring that you make the files sizes of your images and other media as small as possible, *see Section 2.6, page 23.*

The three principles in developing websites are:

- keep it simple – limit the number of web technologies to preferred ones;
- ensure you are standards compliant; and
- minimise the size of your pages.

There are two key web standards **XHMTL** and **CSS** that anyone who is designing and building websites should use by default. Using these two standards will ensure that your websites are easier to maintain. *Section 2.3, page 16 and 2.4, page 19* explain how they work and why you should be using them.

2.2: Standards

The W3C was founded in 1994 by Tim Berners Lee and now has over 450 members consisting of the most important and influential technology organisations from around the world (e.g. Sun Microsystems, BT, Google, Vodafone, AOL). The W3C develops, what it refers to as, **recommendations** of web technologies or **open specifications** that anyone can adopt. However, since the 450 or so members have always adopted the recommendations, they have always become the worldwide 'de facto' standards.

There are considerable benefits to anyone who adheres to W3C standards when developing websites. Documents that adhere to the standards make it easier for any software such as browsers and search engines to understand, making them what is called 'machine readable'. This means your pages will load faster and be more accessible to search engines so your sites are more likely to be listed higher in the search results. Standards are written to be backwards compatible, which means older browsers will still be able to display your pages sensibly. Compliant documents (such as XML) can be converted with greater ease into other formats, e.g. for mobile devices. It also means your pages will be more **accessible,** so voice/braille and text-only browsers will be able to understand your pages, (*see Chapter 11, pages 169–180* for more on accessibility). Your page designs will display consistently, whatever arrangement of computer and software your users may have. Being standards-compliant will also mean that your sites will be easier to maintain since it is easier for different developers to understand the code.

To ensure that your pages are standards-compliant you should use **validation services**. These are usually web-based applications that can be used to check web pages against the standards and will generate a list of errors they find in your code. The W3C has the most popular validation services, which can be found at **http://validator.w3.org**. Once your website is free of errors, you can, if you wish, display the appropriate **conformance icons** on your pages to show that your site is standards-compliant. You may also include a hyperlink back to the validation service so that users can check for themselves.

Figure 2.1: Conformance icons for the W3C validation services for XHTML, CSS and Web Accessibility Initiative

The following sections explain the process of validating your websites for specific standards. The cost of ignoring standards will severely limit the visibility and accessibility of your site, which clearly does not make much sense.

2.3: XHTML

As the World Wide Web has gained in popularity so the number of software tools and 'developers' who create poorly-coded HTML has increased. Web browsers have been developed over time to accommodate and display poorly-coded pages that include errors such as open tags, missing structural tags and incorrectly nested tags (*see Figure 2.2a* for an example of a badly-formed HTML document and *Figure 2.2b* for the corrected version.)

```
<body
<Head>
<p>The first paragraph. <b><i>Welcome</b></i> to the
    badly formed page.
</body>
```

Figure 2.2a: A badly-formed HTML document

```
<html>
<head>
</head>
<body>
<p>The first paragraph. <b><i>Welcome</i></b> to the
    badly formed page.</p>
    </body>
</html>
```

Figure 2.2b: A well-formed HTML document

There are an ever-increasing number of devices that can access the Internet, such as mobile phones and digital televisions. These devices do not have the processing power of a desktop PC and are unable to cope with the variations in coding that an HTML document might have. They require stricter coded documents in order to process the data correctly and faster.

Extensible Hypertext Mark-up Language (XHTML) is a standard created to enable such development. It is based on HTML, but also adheres to the rules and constructs of XML (*see page 27*).

The basic rules of XHTML are:

● all documents have a document declaration (*see page 17*);

● all tags are to be written in lowercase;

● all content must be enclosed with opening and closing tags;

- all attribute values must be quoted;

- attribute minimisation is not allowed;

- all tags must be nested correctly in accordance to the XHTML standard;

- empty tags need a space before the / (e.g. `<br />`

Figure 2.3 shows a well-formed XHTML version of the HTML in *Figure 2.2b*.

```
<!DOCTYPE html PUBLIC "-//W3C//DTD XHTML 1.0
    Transitional//EN" "http://www.w3.org/TR/xhtml1/DTD/
    xhtml1-transitional.dtd">
<html xmlns="http://www.w3.org/1999/xhtml">
<head>
</head>
<body>
<p>The first paragraph. <b><i>Welcome</i></b><br /> to
    a simple XHTML page.</p>
</body>
</html>
```

Figure 2.3: A well-formed XHTML document

XHTML elements

As XHTML is an XML document, it is governed by the rules of XML and these are set out in a document called a **Document Type Definition (DTD)** (*see Section 2.7*).

All XHTML documents must start with a **DOCTYPE** declaration as the first line of the document. The DOCTYPE declaration points to the XHTML DTD and specifies all the correct and permissible tags that can be included in an XHTML document. The specification is located on the W3C website since it defined the XHTML standard in the first place. Here is an example of a complete DOCTYPE declaration:

```
<!DOCTYPE html PUBLIC "-//W3C//DTD XHTML 1.0
    Transitional//EN" "http://www.w3.org/TR/xhtml1/DTD/
    xhtml1-transitional.dtd">
```

Notice that the declaration does not follow the rules for XHTML documents; this is because it is not actually an XHTML tag. The `"-//W3C//DTD XHTML 1.0 Transitional//EN"` part is information about the origin and nature of the standard, for example:

- it is publicly available;

- originates from the W3C;

- is written in English; and

- is the standard for 'XHTML 1.0 Transitional'.

The second part of the DOCTYPE declaration points to the place on the web where the actual DTD can be found.

There are three possible DOCTYPE declarations you could use at the beginning of an XHTML document:

Strict DTD:

```
<!DOCTYPE html PUBLIC "-//W3C//DTD XHTML 1.0 Strict//
    EN" "http://www.w3.org/TR/xhtml1/DTD/xhtml1-strict.
    dtd">
```

Transitional DTD:

```
<!DOCTYPE html PUBLIC "-//W3C//DTD XHTML 1.0
    Transitional//EN" "http://www.w3.org/TR/xhtml1/DTD/
    xhtml1-transitional.dtd">
```

Frameset DTD:

```
<!DOCTYPE html PUBLIC "-//W3C//DTD XHTML 1.0 Frameset//
    EN" "http://www.w3.org/TR/xhtml1/DTD/xhtml1-
    frameset.dtd">
```

Strict is for XHTML documents that do not include any formatting or layout tags like `<font>` or `<table>`, but rely on style sheets instead (*see Section 2.4, page 19* for details).

Transitional is for XHTML documents that use some formatting and layout information.

The **Frameset** is for XHTML documents that use the `<frameset>` tag. However unless you really need to, you should not use this tag because it is difficult to ensure your pages are accessible and search engine optimised. The transitional DTD is the most often used.

When a browser sees the DOCTYPE declaration for XHTML it will follow the rules of the DTD when trying to display the page. If there are any mistakes in the XHTML, it will not try to work out how best to display the page, but will display it with the errors. Web authoring tools, such as Adobe Dreamweaver and Microsoft FrontPage, have options for making pages XHTML compliant. In Dreamweaver MX for instance, you can convert an HTML document to XHTML (transitional) and you can set a default so that all new pages are automatically XHTML compliant.

XHTML documents must then have a `<title>` tag in the `<head>` tag and include the '`xmlns`' attribute. that is a URL to the 'name space' defining all the terms used in XHTML as shown here:

```
<html xmlns="http://www.w3.org/1999/xhtml">
```

Attributes in XHTML must be lower case and values must be in quotes, for example:

`<img SRC=mypic.gif />` should be `<img src="mypic.gif" />`

and they must not be 'minimised', for example:

`<td nowrap>` should be `<td nowrap="nowrap">`.

There are other requirements in making a file XHTML compliant and you should refer to one of the sites listed in *Further reading and research, page 34.*

2.4: Cascading Style Sheets (CSS)

In order to allow designers to be more creative with the look of their web pages, HTML was enhanced to apply different formatting to the text with use of font tags. These can change the font, size and colour of the text. Additional tags such as bold, center and small can also applied to change the appearance.

Adding these types of formatting tags can create a number of issues:

- increased file size due to the additional tags;
- greater chances of malformed tags;
- unable to separate design from content easily;
- longer development time.

Cascading Style Sheets (CSS) were developed to separate design from content and logical document structure. These can be included within an XHTML or HTML document or stored as a separate external file that is referenced by the XHTML or HTML document(s) or even a combination of the two. *Figure 2.3* is an example of an XHTML document with a style sheet added and here is how an external style sheet is referenced from an XHMTL document:

```
<head>
   <link rel="stylesheet" type="text/css"
   href="astylesheet.css" />
</head>
```

The content of the external style sheet will simply contain the style definitions (lines 4–6 in *Figure 2.3*).

> **NOTE**
>
> If all the files on your website were linked to an external CSS, then changing the look of the whole site can be done with just one file rather than changing every file in your site individually, potentially saving hours of work.

CSS syntax

The CSS syntax is made up of three parts: a **selector**, a **property** and a **value**:

selector {property**:** value}, for example:

```
p {font-size:14 pt}
```

Figure 2.4 shows how a style is used to define the format of all paragraphs, i.e. <p> tags in a web page. Styles are placed in the <head> tag so that the style can apply to all <p> tags in the web page. This approach of including the styles in the <head> tag is called **embedded style sheets**. The advantage of this is that to change the appearance of all paragraphs in a single web page only requires changing the style once in the <head> tag.

A **style rule** to format all paragraphs with Arial, 14 point size font (line 6). A style rule consists of at least one **style property**, e.g. 'text-decoration' and a corresponding value, e.g. 'underline' with each style rule separated by a semicolon.

There is another type of style rule called a **style class** (line 7). Style class declarations are preceded by a period and only apply to elements that include that class in its declaration as shown in the second paragraph tag (line 13).

Line 8 shows a third way of defining a style called an **id selector**, which is preceded by a hash. The difference between a style class and an id selector is that a style class may be used by multiple tags but an id selector will only apply to one element.

Figure 2.5 shows what this HTML looks like in a browser; notice that the second paragraph inherits the paragraph style rule, but with the under text decoration added.

```
1   <!DOCTYPE html PUBLIC "-//W3C//DTD XHTML 1.0
    Transitional//EN" "http://www.w3.org/TR/xhtml1/DTD/
    xhtml1-transitional.dtd">
2   <html xmlns="http://www.w3.org/1999/xhtml">
3   <head>
4   <title>Example of a CSS</title>
5   <style>
6      p       {font-size:14 pt;font-family:
       arial,sans-serif;}
7      .upara       {text-decoration: underline;
    background-color: #cccccc;}
8      #center       {text-align: center}
9      </style>
10  </head>
11  <body>
12  <p>A paragraph formatted with a style</p>
13  <p class="upara">A paragraph formatted with a style
    class</p>
14  <p id="center">A paragraph formatted with an id
    selector</p>
15  </body>
16  </html>
```

*Figure 2.4: An XHTML document containing a style
declaration in the <head> tag*

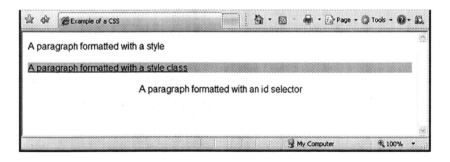

Figure 2.5: The web page produced from the code shown in Figure 2.3

CSS-positioning

CSS-positioning is another important feature of CSS that makes it is possible to define the height, width, visibility and position of a style class. CSS-positioning allows you to position content anywhere in a web page without using the

21

<table> tags. The code in *Figure 2.6* includes the definition of a style called 'layer1' with properties for its position, size and visibility; notice that the style is preceded by a hash ('#') not a period (line 4). To use the new style we need to insert a <span> tag into the body of the document with a reference the new style 'id=layer1' (line 9). Most HTML tags can be included between the <span> tags. If any other <span> tag references the layer1 style class, they will also be placed in the same position so care should be taken.

```
1    <!DOCTYPE html PUBLIC "-//W3C//DTD XHTML 1.0
     Transitional//EN" "http://www.w3.org/TR/xhtml1/DTD/
     xhtml1-transitional.dtd">
2    <html xmlns="http://www.w3.org/1999/xhtml">
2    <head>
3      <style>
4            #layer1 {position:absolute; top:100px;
     left:200px; height:80px;
5            width: 200px; visibility: visible;}
6      </style>
7    </head>
8    <body>
9      <span id="layer1"> I'm here</span>
10   </body>
11 </html>
```

Figure 2.6: Specifying size and position of a style class

There are very good reasons why you should master CSS-positioning and avoiding using tables in your web pages – **tableless web design**:

- tables make web pages very complex and difficult to understand and maintain;

- nested tables (i.e. table tags within table tags) take longer to load;

- tables make web pages less accessible for screen readers (*see Chapter 11, pages 169–180*); and

- pages that use tables do not always print well.

However, there are problems with using CSS-positioning because of the variations between the ways in which different browsers treat them. For this reason, if you check the source code for many of the most visited pages on the web (e.g. the BBC, Google), you will notice that they still use tables for some parts of their site. To be serious about website maintenance you should learn and start using style sheets, and ideally, convert any older websites to CSS. This is only a brief introduction to CSS and you are recommended to find out more about styles is at **www.w3schools.com** or some of the other references at the end of this chapter (*see page 34*).

2.5: Optimisation for browsers

Although many homes and businesses now have fast broadband access to the Internet, people are still impatient, so even a wait of 20 seconds can seem like a long time. Therefore, it is still essential that you optimise your web pages to minimise download times. The first important consideration is to ensure that you stick to the standards to make it easier for browsers to display and then to validate your pages (*see Sections 2.2, page 15* and *2.3, page 16*).

If you are unwilling to move entirely to using CSS-positioning, you can still gain considerable benefits from using CSS to format your pages, but use tables for layout. Using CSS will make web page files smaller since you only need to define a format once instead of using multiple font tags. If you still intend to use tables, avoid using **nested tables**, i.e. placing tables within tables, since this increases the processing that the browser has to do and delays the displaying of the web page.

Other features to avoid in web pages are framesets and Java applets because they create more work for the browser and make pages less accessible. Adobe Flash animations are generally acceptable since Flash files are usually small. However, Flash should only be used sparingly and you must optimise your Flash files.

It is also possible to reduce the size of a web page by removing links that are not used. To monitor which links are not used you will need to have a site monitoring application installed on your web server or use a free service such as **Google Analytics (www.google.com/analytics/)**.

2.6: Image optimisation

Image optimisation can have an enormous impact on the speed that a page downloads. By optimising an image the goal is to reduce the file size, in bytes, but to aim to maintain the image's visual quality so that the images download quickly and look good. Image editing tools such as Adobe PhotoShop or Corel Paint Shop Pro have special features for helping you do this.

The simplest solution is not to use images at all. Ask yourself the question, "Does this image add to the usability or appeal of the page or not?" Images used only to relay textual information, such as headings or buttons, can be replaced by text formatted with CSS. **Animated GIFs** should be avoided if possible since each frame of the file is a separate image so files can become quite large.

The three standard formats used for images in web pages are **Joint Pictures Expert Group (JPEG or JPG)**, **Graphics Interchange Format (GIF)** and **Portable Networks Graphics (PNG)**. In general, use the JPEG format for black and white or colour photographs and GIF or PNG for images that include distinct lines, such as maps, cartoons or that contain text.

Each image format has various parameters that can be adjusted to reduce its size in bytes. This process generally means adjusting the amount of **compression** used, which means recoding or decreasing the number of bits per pixel to reduce an image's size in bytes. Each image format uses different compression techniques or algorithms, but image-editing programs have features for adjusting these parameters (*see Figure 2.7*). Using applications such as Adobe PhotoShop make it easy to adjust the compression of a JPG image from 0 (high compression – low quality) to 100 (low compression – high quality) as shown in *Figure 2.8*.

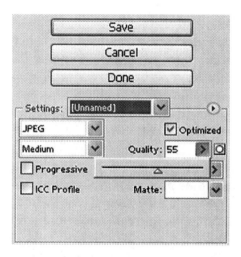

Figure 2.7: Adobe PhotoShop dialogue box for adjusting the compression of a JPG image

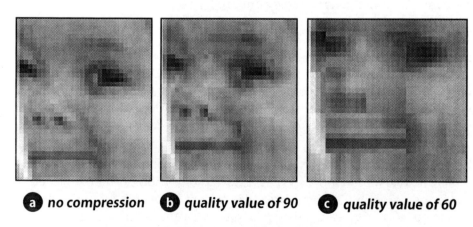

ⓐ *no compression*   ⓑ *quality value of 90*   ⓒ *quality value of 60*

Figure 2.8: The effect of different quality values applied to a jpeg image (the image has been enlarged to 500 percent)

A word of warning, the compression algorithm used in JPG files is **lossy**, i.e. when you increase the level of compression, you literally remove some of the data from the original file permanently. Therefore, it is advisable to keep the original file and save the compressed file under a different name.

There are a number of options for reducing the size of a GIF or PNG image as shown in the Adobe PhotoShop 'Save for Web' dialogue box in *Figure 2.9*. Most image editing tools will have a similar function.

The key way to reduce the file size is to decrease the number of colours used (item ❶ in *Figure 2.8*). Designers systematically reduce the number of colours from 256, checking the quality of image after each reduction, to the point beyond which the quality of the image would be too poor.

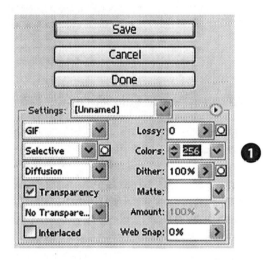

Figure 2.9: Adobe PhotoShop dialogue box for adjusting GIF and PNG-8 image formats

PNG and GIF formats are both based on the idea of a **Colour Look-Up Table – CLUT** or **palette**. Each tiny point in an image is called a pixel (picture-element) and is anything from one to 24 bits (three bytes) in length depending on the image. A one bit pixel can only display two colours – black or white, whereas a 24 bit pixel can display one of 16,777,216 colours. The number of bits per pixel is usually called the **colour depth**. The CLUT is an extra element tagged onto an image file that lists all the colours used in the image. *Figure 2.10*, on the following page, shows an illustration of how a CLUT works. In the first instance, all the colour information is stored with each pixel so three bytes are required for each one ❶. In the second instance, ❷ each pixel refers to the CLUT in ❸ , so for pixel A, instead of storing the 24 bit colour, D8D8D8D, only the location of the colour in the CLUT needs to be stored, i.e. position '0'.

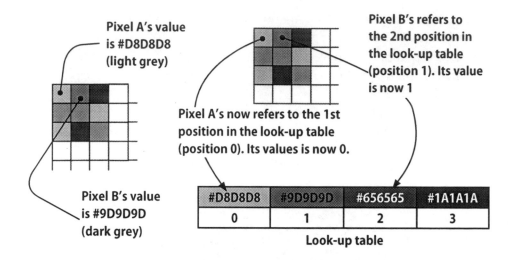

Figure 2.10: Illustration of a Colour Look-Up Table (CLUT)

Now that you have an understanding of CLUTs we can look at how you can optimise the image by modifying the CLUT and reducing the number of colours used to a minimum. You can spend time experimenting with adding or removing colours from the CLUT to reduce its size. However, most image editors, such as PhotoShop, have a useful feature that can semi-automate the process. The drop-down menu ❷ in *Figure 2.9, page 25* lists several types of CLUT, including one called 'adaptive' that scans the colours used in the image and picks the best ones to represent the image in the CLUT. Another is called 'restrictive', which only picks colours that display properly in browsers.

In general, the process of optimising images for displaying in web pages requires experimenting with the settings to achieve a balance of a smaller image file size, but ensuring that the image quality is acceptable.

A useful feature supported by GIFs, PNGs and JPGs is called **Interlaced** or **Progressive** download (item ❸ in *Figure 2.9, page 25*). Selecting this method makes the image display in rough outline before it completely downloads and means users can interact with the web page before the whole page downloads and hence they are less likely to become impatient and leave your site.

Web browsers cache (i.e. temporarily store) all recently used files, including images, from a browsed page. Web browsers will also (unless instructed otherwise) use images with the same name from the cache instead of re-downloading them. This feature is a very important consideration for building fast-loading images. All common elements of a page should use the same image and even where they may vary slightly, like headings, these can be split up into smaller images and the identical bits stored in the cache.

Another important point to remember is to size your images correctly and not rely on the width and height attributes of the `<img>` tag. Using the width and height image attributes can mean that a larger image file than necessary is used or a smaller file is 'stretched' to the right size, but then looks pixelated. One other technique to employ, if it is important to display high quality images, is to use **thumbnail images**, i.e. smaller copies of the full-sized image that users click on to hyperlink to the full sized image.

There are many other things to consider when optimising images and those mentioned above are just some of the key methods. Refer to *Further reading and research, page 34* at the end of this chapter for more help. The list below summarises the most important considerations in optimising images:

- choose the right format for an image, JPGs for photographs, GIFs and PNGs for line drawings and cartoons;

- reduce the resolution of the image to 72 dpi in the final version of the image;

- ensure the size of the image is correct and do not rely on using the width and height attributes; but

- use the width and height attributes to help the browser render the page;

- do not use images if you can use text with CSS instead;

- reduce the colour depth to the minimum acceptable quality in GIFs and PNGs;

- reduce the quality (increase the compression) on JPGs to the minimum quality acceptable;

- avoid using animated GIFs unless absolutely necessary;

- adjust the CLUTs to the minimum number of colours;

- use the Interlaced/Progressive feature to help the page display faster; and

- design your web pages and images with caching in mind.

2.7: Extensible Mark-up Language (XML)

Extensible Mark-up Language (XML) is a method of marking up text with useful and meaningful **elements** (which are XML's posh term for tags) and structure that the author/developer defines themselves. Being able to define your own elements to a formalised structure provides greater control of the text in the ways it can be used, for example during conversion (or transformation) of that data to different formats or having the ability to search for information contained only within a specific set of elements.

XML is a standard that evolved from another standard called **SGML (Standard Generalized Mark-up Language)** which is a very prescriptive mark-up language governed by a document called a **Document Type Definition (DTD)**. A DTD defines how a document **must be** structured.

A very simple example might be that a *Document* can contain a *Title*, the *Title* can only contain text and must be followed by a *Paragraph* and that *Paragraph* could contain a *List* that can contain *List Item(s)*. This would prevent an author from inserting a hyperlink in the *Title* or placing another *Title* after the first one. The element mark-up might look like this:

```
<document>
<title>An example title</title>
<p>Paragraph text containing a list
<list>
<list item>I'm a list item</list item>
</list>
</p>
</document>
```

The SGML document would be parsed (checked/validated) against the DTD and rejected if there were any structural errors. You can imagine a DTD can become very large and restrictive and minor changes to the structure, say for example, the addition of an element can create major problems.

The W3C devised XML to be as flexible or restrictive as necessary, but at its simplest, it still retains structure and rules. If you require strict rules for your document structure then a DTD can still be used or a **Schema** (which act in a similar way to DTDs, but are gradually replacing them especially for web developments – *see page 32*) or at its simplest a **well-formed** XML document, i.e. it conforms to the XML standard's syntax rules namely:

- documents must have a root element (first line, *Figure 2.11*);
- elements must have a closing tag;
- the tags are case sensitive;
- elements must be nested correctly;
- attribute values must always be quoted.

Figure 2.11 is an example of a well-formed XML document that shows how we could have the details of a product for purchase:

```
1    <?xml version="1.0" encoding="ISO-8859-1"?>
2    <list>
3    <prod>
4    <prod-name id="1">XRN2 MP3 player</prod-name>
5    <prod-description>1 Gb of memory</prod-description>
6    <prod-price>£45</prod-price>
7    </prod>
9    <prod>
10   <prod-name id="2">Big MP3 player</prod-name>
11   <prod-description> Cool looking device in chrome</
     prod-description>
12   <prod-price>£75</prod-price>
13   </prod>
14   </list>
```

Figure 2.11: An example of a simple well-formed XML file

New tags may be added whenever you require them (hence the 'eXtensible'). XML provides a description and structure of the content, but contains no formatting information. Therefore, in order for XML to be used in web pages it needs to be transformed into a browser compatible structure such as XHTML (which is, itself an XML document) or linked with a cascading style sheet (see page 31).

XSL transformations

There are several ways of transforming XML documents, one of which is the transformation language for XML called the **XML Stylesheet Language (XSL)**, created by the W3C. XSL actually consists of several different mark-up languages and it is the **XSL Transformations (XSLT)** language part that 'transforms' XML documents into other types of document, in particular XHTML. *Figure 2.12* shows an example of how an XSLT file can transform the XML in *Figure 2.11* into XHTML.

All XSLT documents begin with some standard declarations ❶. The statement at ❷ is the start of an XSLT template that defines how the XML file will be transformed into XHTML and is closed at statement ❼. XSLT may have more than one template tag. XHTML statements can be defined inside an XSLT template, e.g. the statement at ❹ says 'search through the XML and find all instances of XML tags nested inside the `<prod>` tag'. Then the three statements at ❺ define how each tag will be transformed; the first and second statements makes no changes to the 'prod-name' tag; and the third applies the style declaration in the `<div>` tag to all "prod-price XML tags. The statement at ❻ says loop through the whole XML document to find all instances of the listed tags.

```
1  <?xml version="1.0" encoding="ISO-8859-1"?>
2  <xsl:stylesheet version="1.0" xmlns:xsl="http://
   www.w3.org/1999/XSL/Transform" xmlns="http://www.
   w3.org/TR/xhtml1/strict">
   <xsl:template match="/">
3  <html>
   <body>
4  <xsl:for-each select="list/prod">
          <xsl:value-of select="prod-name"/>
5     {   <xsl:value-of select="prod-description"/>
          <xsl:value-of select="prod-price"/>
       <div style="text-decoration: underline">
       </div>
6  </xsl:for-each>
   </body>
   </html>
   </xsl:template>
7  </xsl:stylesheet>
```

Figure 2.12: An example of an XSLT file

The XML file needs to link to the XSLT file with a statement like this at the beginning:

```
<?xml-stylesheet type="text/xsl" href="style.xsl"?>
```

The output of the XML file in *Figure 2.11* with the XSLT file in *Figure 2.12* would look like this:

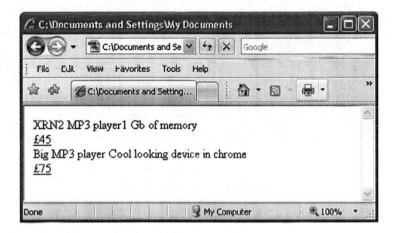

It may seem like a lot of effort to produce a web page that you could simply create in XHTML and CSS. However, XSLT is very powerful and can be used to transform any XML document into many other formats such as comma or tab delimited formats (csv files) or **XHTML Basic** for displaying on a small screen such as a mobile phone. XSLT can be compared more to a programming language than a mark-up language in that it can carry out computations, for instance changing the order of elements in a document or substituting one word for another. This is only a very brief introduction to XSLT and you are advised to refer to one of the references at the end of this chapter (*see page 34*) to discover the full potential of XML and XSLT.

Using CSS with XML

Another way of using XML documents is to link them to a CSS as described in *Section 2.4, page 19. Figure 2.13* shows an example of a CSS that formats the XML data, shown in *Figure 2.11* and *Figure 2.14* shows the result. The first line of the style sheet makes it possible to position each XML element on the page.

```
prod, prod-name, prod-description, prod-price {
    display: block }
prod { font-family: sans-serif; background: gray;
    color: white }
prod-name{ margin: 1em; color: yellow }
prod-description{ text-align: center; margin-bottom:
    2em }
prod-price { line-height: 1.5; margin-left: 15%
```

Figure 2.13: Style sheet used to format the XML document in Figure 2.14

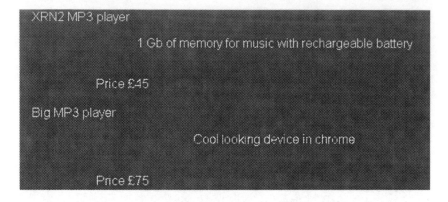

XRN2 MP3 player

1 Gb of memory for music with rechargeable battery

Price £45

Big MP3 player

Cool looking device in chrome

Price £75

**Figure 2.14: The web page produced from the XML in Figure 2.11
and the style sheet in Figure 2.13**

For more information on using CSS with XML see *Further reading, page 34.*

Even though you can invent any element you like in XML, there are situations when it is useful to restrict the elements to an agreed set. For example, many websites that are frequently updated with content such as news headlines use 'RSS' web-feeds. Since there are many different applications that use the RSS web-feeds, it is important that they all adhere to the same format. For this reason, the W3C developed **XML schema** documents for defining a restricted set of XML tags for a specific purpose. Many XML schemas have already been developed including those used for defining:

- **mathematical symbols** – MathML;
- **learning content** – IMS; and for delivering
- **multimedia content** – SMIL (Synchronised Multimedia Integration Language).

Note

XHTML is actually written in XML and has its own XML schema. To find out more about XML schema please refer to the references at the end of the chapter.

XML is ideal to use in situations where:

- the content is highly structured, for example a catalogue of goods for an online shop;
- there is a need for a common format between specific web-based applications such as mathematical symbols;
- output is likely to be required in multiple formats, e.g. for web pages, mobile phones and Portable Document Format (PDF) files; and
- the content needs to be changed programmatically, e.g. replacing key words within specific elements.

A good example of a real-world use of XML is the UK Government's **e-Government Interoperability Framework (e-GIF)** initiative that uses an XML schema to facilitate exchange of content between government departments and for the presentation of information to the public via the web. More on e-GIF initiative can be found in *Further reading and research, page 34.*

2.8: Chapter summary

Web technologies continue to evolve rapidly; what was considered good practice a few years ago has now been displaced by newer technologies and techniques. Building websites that are easier to maintain, means that you should build them using XHTML and CSS. You should also make an effort to ensure your web pages are standards-compliant so that they are accessible to the greatest number of people, browsers and devices. Optimising web pages means ensuring that pages download quickly and are easy to use. This means ensuring images are kept to a minimum number and are optimised for size in bytes. It also means using CSS-positioning rather than tables and avoiding using framesets or nested tables. XML and XSLT are powerful new technologies that can be used to produce documents of different formats and provides the opportunity for agreed formats of content, in particular applications such as the UK Government's e-GIF initiative.

2.9: Example questions

1. What changes do you think need to be made to web pages made in HTML to improve their speed of download, appearance and compatibility with different browsers?

2. A photography company wants to display a portfolio of its work on its website. Advise the company on what it needs to consider to ensure its portfolio of work looks good on the web.

3. Give an overview of XML and reasons why it is useful.

2.10: Example answers

1. The objective of this question is to ascertain how much you know about newer web technologies, e.g. XHTML and CSS, and what you know about optimising web pages. You should start by explaining the importance of sticking to the W3C standards and then you should give a brief overview of XHTML and CSS and explain why web pages made with HTML should be converted to XHTML. You should finish your answer by noting the other changes you can make to web pages to make the download quicker, for example using CSS –positioning instead of tables and avoiding the use of nested tables.

2. This question is all about optimising images for displaying on the web. You need to explain the different image formats and the types of images they should be used for (JPGs best for photographs, GIFs/PNGs for line drawings and cartoons). You should then explain the need to make image

files on the web smaller in bytes so that they display quickly. Making image files smaller means reducing their quality, which a photography company might not be so happy with, therefore you could suggest using thumbnail images linked to the full-sized image, perhaps warning site visitors about the size of the full-sized image. You should explain the process of reducing the file size to the point when the image quality is still acceptable to the human eye. The process is different for JPGs and GIFs and PNGs. JPGs can be compressed, but the quality will be reduced; GIFs and PNGs can be reduced in size by changing the colour depth and reducing the number of colours in the CLUT. You might want to suggest that they add interlaced and progressive download so that users can see images sooner.

3. Start by explaining the drawback of mixing formatting information with content in XHTML or HTML and then explain the benefits of separating the two. Use a simple example to show how XML is free of formatting information and then explain how XSLT and CSS can be used to format the raw XML into a web page. Finish by giving the situations in which XML is a preferred solution, e.g. common format for data exchange, output in multiple formats.

2.11: Further reading and research

Websites

Add the number in square brackets to **www.bookref.net/lpwm** for the most up to date web link, for example www.bookref.net/lpwm0110

www.w3schools.com – this site contains many useful tutorials on XHTML and CSS and other web development techniques. [0201]

www.webreference.com/dev/graphics/ – is a tutorial on optimising images for web pages. [0202]

http://validator.w3.org/ – validator for XHTML. [0203]

http://jigsaw.w3.org/css-validator/ – validator for CSS. [0204]

www.webmonkey.com/webmonkey/design/site_building/tutorials/ tutorial2.html – is a tutorial for optimising a site. [0205]

http://w3tableless.com – is an automatic validation service for tableless web design. [0206]

http://glish.com/css/ includes advice and tutorials on using CSS and tableless web design. [0207]

www.egifcompliance.org/towards.cfm – brief overview of the UK Government's e-GIF initiative. [0208]

Books

Cunliffe, D and Elliott, G. (2005) *Multimedia Computing*, Lexden Publishing: Colchester.

Gandy, E and Stobart, G. (2005) *JavaScript: Creating Dynamic Web Pages*, Lexden Publishing: Colchester.

Chapter 3

WEB SERVERS

Chapter overview

This chapter explains what web servers are and do and then considers the main technologies associated with them.

Learning outcomes

After studying this chapter and answering the example questions at the end of the chapter on *page 50*, you should be able to achieve these outcomes:

Outcome 1: Describe the functions of a web server.

Outcome 2: Describe the main web server technologies.

Outcome 3: Compare the two most commonly used web servers.

How will you be assessed on this?

A tutor will want to know that you are familiar with the functions of a web server and is unlikely to be satisfied with a brief answer. The topic of web servers is likely to be the focus of one or more exam questions. In coursework, you might be expected to find out what you can about different web server applications and compare them. You might also be asked to find out what other functions web servers perform beyond the core ones mentioned here or in class.

3.1: The web

The web has now become an essential medium for all sorts of transactions in life, buying and selling, advertising, keeping up to date with your friends and family, studying, etc. In this section we look at the events that occur when someone clicks on a hyperlink on a computer running a web browser.

Figure 3.1 illustrates how the web works. The web uses its own protocol to transfer data called **Hypertext Transfer Protocol (HTTP)**, which in turn uses the Internet Protocol Suite – **TCP/IP** (*see Chapter 4, pages 53–74*). Currently there are two versions of HTTP, 1.0 and 1.1. The web uses its own format for data called **Hypertext Mark-up Language (HTML)**, web browsers read HTML and follow its instructions to display the page (see *Further reading and research, page 52* on HTML). When a person clicks on a hyperlink in a web page using a web browser program, such as Microsoft's Internet Explorer (*Figure 3.1* ❶), to display a web page that is located on another computer on the Internet, it needs to make a request to that computer. The hyperlink should be a URL that contains: the name of the destination computer, the directory path and filename.

Figure 3.1 shows how a request is made. The client ❶ sends out an **HTTP request** ❷ for the data. An HTTP request contains information about what data is required and the addresses of the sender and destination. The HTTP request is converted into TCP/IP data packets and sent over the Internet ❸, eventually arriving at the computer with the required information ❹. Only computers running applications called **HTTP/web servers** are able to despatch web files across the Internet. The HTTP/web server works out which data is required and sends back an **HTTP response** ❺ over the Internet ❸ which also contains the address of the sender and its destination. When the browser of the requesting computer ❶ receives the HTTP response ❺, it reads the HTML contained in its data and attempts to display it in the browser window.

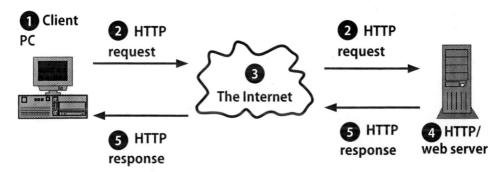

Figure 3.1: How the web works

HTML is text-based, although web pages often include many other media types, such as images, sound and video. To enable HTTP to deal with other media types, a set of defined media types called **MIME-types** have been established.

MIME stands for **Multipurpose Mail Extensions**, but they apply to the web as well as e-mail. Common MIME-types include 'image/jpeg' to denote the data is a JPEG image, 'video/x-msvideo' to denote the data is a Microsoft AVI video file and 'application/x-shockwave-flash' to indicate that the data is an Adobe Flash file. So an HTTP response might contain other types of media data other than text. When the browser reads the HTTP response it works out whether it can display the data for each of the MIME-types identified; if it cannot, it will either ignore it or put up an error message. So the support of MIME-types in HTTP allows multimedia web pages to be constructed. Some MIME-types, such as the one for Adobe Flash, require a **plugin** or helper program to be able to display them in the browser. Browsers often have several plugins installed – one for sound file formats, one for video file formats and one for proprietary media types such as Flash, etc.

3.2:   HTTP requests and responses

In this section we examine the contents of the HTTP request and the response in more detail. An HTTP request or response is made up of the following:

- an initial line;
- zero or more header lines;
- a blank line; and
- an optional message body (e.g. a file or HTML data).

The initial line is different for a request than for response. The **initial request line** defines the method name, the local path of the requested resource, and the version of HTTP being used. A typical example would be:

`GET /path to file/home.htm HTTP/1.0`

The two main methods are **GET** and **POST**, GET means "I want this resource" and the POST method means that the client browser is sending something extra to the server to be processed, such as the contents of a form. The 'path to file' is the directory on the web server where the resource requested resides.

The initial response line or **status line** defines the status of the request and is made up of:

- the version of HTTP used;
- the **status code** of the request for the benefit of programs; and
- a short phrase describing the status code for the benefit of human readers.

A typical example of an initial response line would be:

`HTTP/1.0 200 OK`

The most common status codes are shown in *Figure 3.2* although there are many more and these can be found in *Further reading and research, page 52.*

200 OK	The request completed successfully.
404 Not Found	The requested resource doesn't exist.
301 Moved Permanently	The requested resource has been assigned to a new permanent URL.
302 Moved Temporarily	The requested resource resides temporarily under a different URL.
500 Server Error	The server encountered an unexpected condition that prevented it from fulfilling the request.

Figure 3.2: Common HTTP response status codes

The header lines are made up of a name, a colon and a value and there are many different name-value pairs that can be used. *Figure 3.3* shows typical name and value header pairs in an HTTP request and response. HTTP 1.0 defines 16 headers and HTTP 1.1 defines 64 headers, a full list of them can be found in *Further reading and research, page 52*. *Figure 3.3* also shows the HTML document requested appended to the HTTP response header.

GET /path/file.html HTTP/1.0
From: someone@somewhere.com
User-Agent: HTTPTool/1.0
[blank line here]
	HTTP/1.1 200 OK
	Connection: close
	Date: Wed, 14 Jan 2004 06:38:49 GMT
	Server: Microsoft-IIS/4.0
	Content-Length: 37272
	Content-Type: text/html
	Client-Response-Num: 1
	
	`<html>`
	`<body>`
	`contents of home.htm document`
	`</body>`
	`</html>`

(a)	(b)

Figure 3.3: Typical HTTP header for (a) HTTP request and
(b) HTTP response with associated HTML document

3.3: Web servers in detail

So far, we have talked about web servers in general terms, in this section we examine the concept of a web server as a program and what it can do.

It is often confusing when people refer to **web servers**. Are they referring to a program or a computer? The answer is that a web server is both a program and a computer. It is possible to run a web server program on most personal computers – web developers often have one running on their own computer to see what their website looks like running through HTTP. There are many different web server programs available; the most common are Internet Information Server (IIS) from Microsoft, Apache (an open source web server from the Apache Software Foundation) and the Java System Web Server (formerly called Sun ONE) from Sun Microsystems. Most web servers share a common set of functions, but may also have some that are unique to that software.

> **TIP**
>
> Go to the Apache Foundation website (**www.apache.org**), download and install a copy of Apache for either Windows or Unix (depending on your operating system) onto your computer. If you are running Windows 98 or ME, you can install the Microsoft Personal Web Server, which is a cut-down version of IIS, from your Windows installation CD. If you are running Windows 2000 or XP professional, you should have IIS available on the installation CD. Unfortunately, neither PWS or IIS is easily available for Windows XP home edition.

All web server programs should have facilities that enable them to administer and control a number of key functions. When an HTTP request is made for a document, that document may be located in a number of places, for example in a directory on the same hard drive on which the web server is installed, on a different drive but on the same computer or even on a different computer. Therefore, the web server program must 'know' and be capable of accessing different computers and locations. In addition, a web server program may handle requests for sub-domains for that domain name, for instance **www.pembrokeshire.ac.uk** and **online.pembrokeshire.ac.uk** could be both hosted by the same web server program with each domain having its own IP address. In this case, a web server program is acting as a **virtual server** for a particular domain. It is also possible to configure the web server so that an address and path, such as **www.pembrokeshire.ac.uk/staff/**, points to a different hard drive or computer and directory from that indicated in the URL, using what are called **aliases**.

Managing a website can be handled in different ways; some web server programs, such as IIS, have an interface called a **management console** that enables changes to be made to the web server program as shown in *Figure 3.4, page 40*. The management console can either run as a conventional application or for some web server programs it can be accessed via a web page interface instead. Some web servers, for example Apache, are controlled by editing a text based configuration file that Apache looks at first when it starts up. Once the server is running, the Apache web server can be controlled by executing commands at the command prompt to change the parameters of the web server program. For example, the line below is a command that will cause Apache to load an optional program module called 'status_module' in order to provide the web server administrator with information on server activity and performance:

```
c:\apache apache -c "LoadModule status_module modules/
    status_mod.so"
```

Web server programs generally include utilities to enable **performance monitoring**. This means how much system resource each website is utilising at any point in time. There are also separate operating system programs designed to undertake performance monitoring. Some web server programs can also control the bandwidth of certain pages in a process called **throttling**. *Figure 3.5* shows the performance monitor for IIS.

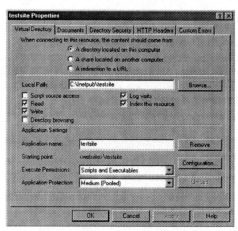

Figure 3.4: IIS management console. The properties of the folder 'testsite' are being examined in the dialogue box

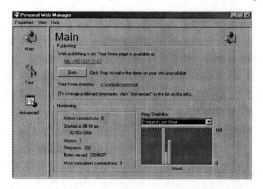

Figure 3.5: Performance monitor for IIS showing the activity of the server in the bottom right of the window

Another important function that web server programs can perform is to act as a **proxy server**. *Figure 3.6* shows a typical proxy server set up. A proxy server sits between the client-computers ❶ and any destination web server ❸ from which a request has been made. The proxy server passes the request ❷ onto the destination web server and receives the response back from it ❸, before passing on the requested document onto the client computer ❶. The proxy server keeps copies, or **caches**, of all requested documents. When the document is requested again, the proxy server can provide the document from its cache without having to make another request to the destination web server. This approach can significantly reduce the amount of time it takes to execute an HTTP request particular for frequently requested documents. The proxy server will cache documents for a defined period of time, for example seven days, and then make a new request to the destination server when the document is next requested. Some proxy servers also monitor who is requesting particular documents and can block access to particular websites.

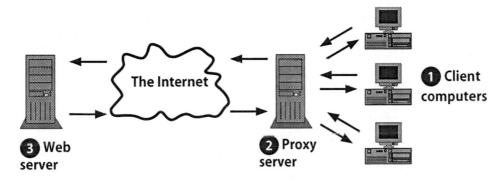

Figure 3.6: A web server ❷ working as a proxy server

Activity logging

Another key function of web server programs is to log activity, including requests for documents and any errors that have occurred. Web server programs record events such as HTTP requests in log files; *Figure 3.7* shows a fragment from a typical log file. Unfortunately, web server programs do nothing more than log activity and do not provide any facilities for analysing activity. However, third party applications can be installed that can analyse the log files and produce tables and charts that summarise activity on the web server, which might include statistics about the number of times a page is accessed, browser types, visitors' operating systems, referring links to the site, country of origin, download errors, etc.

Analysis of the log files is useful when configuring web servers. For example, if the analysis indicates that a particular website is receiving many requests, it may require additional resources.

```
2007-02-12 07:47:08 127.0.0.1 - W3SVC1 001G7-1-LPT04A
127.0.0.1 80 GET /IISHelp/ - 302 0 287 498 0 HTTP/1.1
localhost Mozilla/5.0+(Windows;+U;+Windows+NT+5.0;+en-
GB;+rv:1.8.1.1)+Gecko/20061204+Firefox/2.0.0.1

2007-02-12 07:47:08 127.0.0.1 - W3SVC1 001G7-1-
LPT04A 127.0.0.1 80 GET /IISHelp/iis/misc/default.
asp - 200 0 0 519 15 HTTP/1.1 localhost Mozilla/
5.0+(Windows;+U;+Windows+NT+5.0;+en-GB;+rv:1.8.1.1)+Gecko/
20061204+Firefox/2.0.0.1

2007-02-12 07:47:08 127.0.0.1 - W3SVC1 001G7-1-
LPT04A 127.0.0.1 80 GET /IISHelp/iis/misc/navbar.
asp - 200 0 0 574 0 HTTP/1.1 localhost Mozilla/
5.0+(Windows;+U;+Windows+NT+5.0;+en-GB;+rv:1.8.1.1)+Gecko/
20061204+Firefox/2.0.0.1
```

Figure 3.7: A portion of an IIS log file showing that three HTTP requests were made on the 12-2-07

In addition to static HTML documents, web server programs can support the execution of programs and scripts to produce dynamic content. A simple example would be to present the date and time on a web page when requested from the server (that is the date and time at the server-side not the client-side). *Chapter 5, pages 75–92* explains the way web servers support **dynamic content**.

3.4: Website security

Website security is an important area of website management so it is crucial that you know what this area involves and what measures need to be taken.

The two elements of website security are:

i) controlling access to the website; and

ii) securing HTTP request and response transactions across the Internet.

There are essentially three ways in which web server programs control access to a website:

1. limit access to certain IP addresses or conversely refuse access to certain IP addresses;

2. use **authentication** to limit access; and

3. control the types of actions allowed on a particular website, e.g. execute script or read documents.

Controlling access

A typical example of limiting access to IP addresses is shown in *Figure 3.8* where IIS is being used to prevent access from the IP address 218.234.19.1. The website administrator must first decide if, by default, all IP addresses will be granted access to the website or whether they will be denied. Once this decision has been made, exceptions to this rule can be defined either to grant or deny access to individual IP addresses or ranges of addresses respectively.

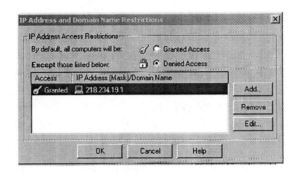

Figure 3.8: IIS configured to prevent access from the IP address 218.234.19.1

Authentication means that the user is required to enter a valid user ID and password when trying to access a website. *Figure 3.9* shows a typical authentication challenge to a user allowing a page to be displayed. Websites that are designed for general public access have a default account pre-configured so that anonymous access to the site can be made. When a request is made for a document, the anonymous account is used automatically unbeknown to the user. Authentication is generally tied up with the way an organisation's network is set up and web server programs are generally configured to accept the users' corporate user id and password.

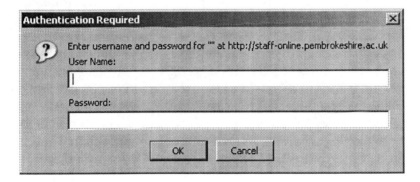

Figure 3.9: A typical web page authentication challenge

Finally, it is also possible to configure a website to limit the types of actions that are allowed. The IIS dialogue box, shown in *Figure 3.4*, also allows the web server administrator to permit the following actions:

- read documents;
- write to the website;
- run scripts (such as ASP – *see Chapter 5, pages 75–92*);
- execute programs.

Secure web server transactions

The second element of website security is the securing of web server transactions over the Internet. The most common method utilised is called the **secure socket layer (SSL)**. SSL is a protocol that encrypts any transaction between the client computer and the web server. Encryption means converting messages into a form that cannot be understood unless you have the means to decipher it. SSL utilises public key cryptography that uses two encryption 'keys' to ensure the transactions are secure:

- a public key that the server can give to any user that requests it; and

- a private key that only the server has access to.

A key is a code that, when applied to any digital message, such as an HTML document, encrypts it, i.e. scrambles it, and makes it meaningless unless you have the right key and means to decrypt it. In addition to the keys, SSL involves **digital certificates** that are issued by a **certificate authority (CA)**, for example those issued by Verisign. The purpose of a digital certificate is to prove that the server establishing the secure connection is what it says it is and the certificate authority is a trusted third party that confirms that the owner of the digital certificate is what it says it is. The digital certificate contains the server's public key.

Figure 3.10 shows how SSL works: in ❶ the client browser establishes a connection with the server indication that a secure connection is required. When the server receives this request it sends the client its digital certificate and its public key ❷; the client and the server agree the appropriate level of security ❸; the client then generates a session key, encrypts it using the server's public key and sends it to the server ❹; any message encrypted with the server's public key is secure because only the server's private key can decrypt it. Now that the server has the client's session key the secure connection can be established ❺ and the client and server can communicate securely using the session key. The initial request for a secure connection is indicated by a secure URL via the protocol **HTTPS** rather than HTTP for example:

https://www.securesite.com

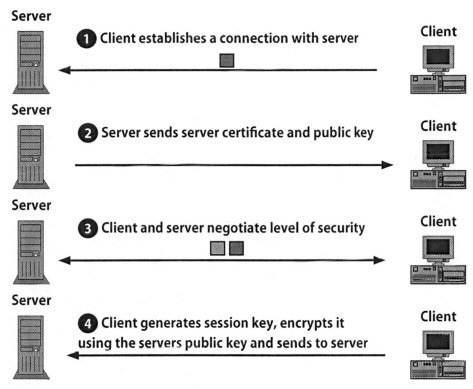

*Figure 3.10: How a server and client establish
a secure connection using SSL*

3.5: Web servers as hardware

In this section, we look at the types of hardware that are used for hosting websites.

Most modern computers are capable of hosting and running a web server program. However, websites that are important to the organisation and those that handle a high number of requests need to run on computers with a higher specification than a conventional desktop PC. The three key questions needed to be asked when specifying a computer to run a website are:

• What will be average level of requests and what will they peak at?

• How critical is it that the website continues to operate all the time?

• Does the website deal mainly with requests that read from hard disks or requests that write to hard disks?

The first question concerns the capacity of the server computer to deal with many requests rapidly and simultaneously. This depends on the kind of **network interface card (NIC)** that is installed to handle the level of website requests. NICs are installed in computers to connect them to a network. The greater the level of traffic, the higher the bandwidth the card must be able to handle. A basic NIC designed for a PC will handle 10–100 Mega bits per second (Mbps) of traffic whereas NICs designed to be used in a web server computer can handle 500–1,000 Mbps, i.e. up to 100 times the bandwidth. There are more details about networks in *Chapter 4, pages 53–74*. Often multiple NICs are installed to work in tandem in server computers. The greater the number and frequency of requests, the higher the specification of the computer used. This means high specification motherboards with powerful processors, greater memory capacity and faster hard disk drives. The usual types of hard disk drive installed in PCs are **Intelligent Drive Electronics (IDE)** or **Enhanced IDE (EIDE)** which have date transfer rates of between 16–100 Mbps. The drives usually used in computers running web servers are **Redundant Array of Independent Disks (RAID)**. RAID disks are made up of an array of two or more hard drives. The data in a file is split into chunks in a process called stripping and then distributed across the disks in the array. The advantage of this approach is that when a file is being read from a RAID disk, multiple simultaneous reads can be made to assemble the file from the strips making access times very quick. A typical RAID disk is capable of transfer rates of up to 400 Mbps.

To ensure websites that are critical to an organisation remain operational, the hardware should be designed to be **fault tolerant**, i.e. a means to continue working if any component hardware or software fails. One of the main techniques of ensuring fault tolerance is to duplicate critical component hardware often referred to as **redundancy**. NICs used in server computers are often made up of multiple 'virtual' NICs. This not only increases the bandwidth of a NIC, but it means if one of the 'virtual' NICs fails the others can continue to operate and ensure continuity of service. RAID drives not only increase access speeds, but they are also designed with fault tolerance and redundancy in mind so that if one of the disks in the array fails the data is retrievable from one of the other disks in the array. If an error is made when either writing or reading data, the in-built error correction ensures that the data can be automatically corrected. Motherboards used for running websites are also designed to be fault tolerant with critical components, such as the processor or sometimes the whole board, duplicated.

The third question of whether the website will be mostly read from rather than written to affects the types of hard drives used. There are various levels of RAID configuration available offering varying degrees of fault tolerance, speed of read and speed of write to disk. When specifying a server computer it is important to have an idea of the kind of usage it will have so that the right level of RAID drive is used. RAID 0 is very fast on reads and writes, but has no fault tolerance. RAID 5 is the most commonly used, offering good access times with fault tolerance, but is not so good on activities that require a lot of writes to disk.

3.6: Web server comparisons

A crucial decision that organisations must make concerns the web server application and platform on which to base its websites. There are many web server applications to choose from, each with its preferred platform. In this section we compare the two main web server applications, **Microsoft IIS** and **Apache,** that account for the vast majority of website installations across the world.

Apache is free **open source** software from the Apache Software Foundation and includes the source files. The availability of the free source code has spurred on the development of Apache functionality by volunteer developers from all around the world. An advantage of Apache is that its components are modular, which means that users can select the components they require. Another advantage of being free is the speed with which bugs are fixed. **IIS** is a Microsoft Windows product and integrates with other Windows products, but is not technically free since it is bundled with all Microsoft's server software, which must be purchased. Apache is administered via a configuration file and the command line; IIS, on the other hand, is administered through a graphical user interface. IIS's integration with Windows means that it also integrates with Windows operating system functions such as directory services, the Windows performance monitor and user management.

Apache was originally developed for the Unix operating system, but is now available for Windows and OS2, whereas IIS is only available for specific versions of Windows such as Windows Server 2000. Both Apache and IIS support basic security features to restrict access by domain name, IP address, user and group. However, IIS also integrates with other Windows security features.

IIS is the more obvious choice if an organisation's PCs and network are already Windows-based. The problem with this approach is that it locks the organisation into Microsoft. If an organisation would prefer not to be locked in to a particular vendor and is already using Unix, then Apache is probably the right choice. However, there is no one person or organisation to turn to when there is a problem with open source products, so it is important an organisation has sufficient expertise in-house to support any open source product. Some companies, for example IBM, do provide support for Unix, but charge for it. About 67% of web servers, worldwide, use Apache and about 20% use Microsoft.

3.7: Web server optimisation

Web servers need to be optimised to ensure content is delivered to a client browser as efficiently and quickly as possible (see *Chapter 2, pages 13–34.*) The factor that can have the biggest effect on web server performance is the caching of web pages and other page objects such as images as outlined in *Section 3.3, page 39*. It is possible to increase control over the way in which web servers and proxy servers cache web pages using information in the HTTP header. HTTP 1.1 defines a number of directives in a response header that can be used by the software controlling the cache. The two most useful of these directives are **Expires**, which defines how long a cache application may keep a copy of the web page, for example:

Expires: Wed, 02 Nov 2007 16:00:00 GMT

The other is the **Entity tag (ETag)** directive that is a unique code generated by a web server each time a web page changes. The cache software checks to see if the ETag has changed since last time, if not it uses the cached copy. A typical Etag may look like this:

```
ETag: "1c722384800bbdf01e1f840d8a642f55"
```

The software that controls the cache follows a set of rules in order to work out if it can use a cached copy:

- If the web page's header tell the cache not to keep the object, it will not.

- If the web page is secure (via HTTPS), it will not be cached.

- A cached page is considered '**fresh**' (that is, able to be sent to a browser without checking with the web server) if It has an expires time set, and is still within the fresh period.

- Fresh web pages are sent directly from the cache, without checking with the originating web server.

- If a page is stale, the cache asks the web server to **validate** the page, or tell the cache whether the copy that it has is still good.

Both IIS and Apache enable the web master to set the header directives. *Figure 3.11* shows the IIS dialogue box for a defining the HTTP header for either a whole site, folder, a special web page or other object. web masters just need to decide when the object should expire, then IIS works out what date to include in the Expires directive.

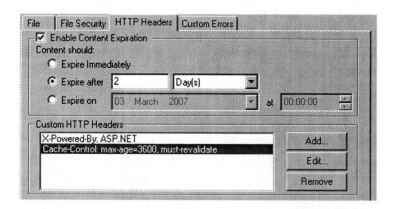

Figure 3.11: The IIS dialogue box for defining the expires header directive and other custom HTTP headers

To define HTTP headers for content on an Apache server you must edit the **.htaccess** text file that is found in each directory of content and add the appropriate headers. *Figure 3.12* shows an example of an .htaccess file with an Expires directive set to one month from the time the file was accessed.

ExpiresActive On
ExpiresDefault "access plus 1 month"

Figure 3.12: .HTACCESS file to set the Expires directive in a HTTP Response header. The Apache module mod_expires must be turned on first

HTTP 1.1 includes the option to compress files sent between a web server and a client browser. The advantage of compressing files in an HTTP exchange is that the compressed files will require fewer IP packets to transfer and, therefore, will be quicker. All latest generation browsers support HTTP compression and will send the following line in the HTTP request to the server:

`Accept-Encoding: gzip`

and the server will include a header indicating that the content has been compressed:

`Content-Encoding: gzip`

IIS has a dialogue box for controlling HTTP compression as shown in *Figure 3.13*.

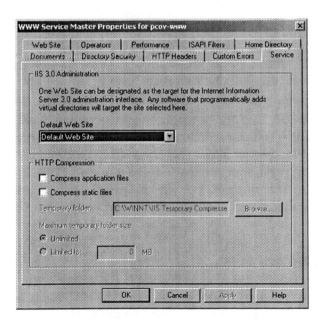

Figure 3.13: IIS dialogue box for setting the HTTP compression options

On Apache servers a module called **mod_deflate** must be installed and the following directive in one of the Apache configuration files called **access.conf** must be added:

```
CompressContent Yes
```

You can check to see if your web server is compressing content at one of the sites listed in *Further reading and research, page 52.*

An important feature of HTTP is the **Keep-alive** function that maintains the TCP connection between a browser and a server over the Internet. Normally HTTP is **stateless**, which means when a browser and server make an HTTP Request and Response, the server forgets all about the browser. So, the next time the same browser makes a request to the server a new TCP connection across the Internet must be established. If a web server has HTTP Keep-alive switched on, it means that the browser and the server use the same TCP connection for multiple HTTP requests/responses. To switch HTTP Keep-alive in IIS there is simple checkbox in the server properties dialogue box. For Apache, an extra directive must be added to the configuration file.

There is a range of other measures that web masters can implement to improve the performance of a web server including adding third party applications. Some of the web sites listed at the end of this chapter provide more details.

3.8: Example questions

1. Explain what happens when a person browsing a web page clicks on a hyperlink whose target destination is www.microsoft.com, but the message says that the page cannot be found?

2. You are the web master of a college which has a web server computer that is a few years old and probably needs upgrading. Whilst you consider upgrading the web server computer you also reflect on what functions the college requires of it to help decide which web server software could provide the right functionality for the college. Write a requirements specification that outlines the type of server hardware you recommend and the functions you anticipate you will need from the web server software.

3.9: Example answers

1. This question is trying to ascertain what you know about HTTP and the interactions between a client browser and the HTTP/web server. Crucially, the question is asking what happens in an HTTP transaction. Begin by explaining that a hyperlink in a web page to an external resource should contain the full URL prefixed by HTTP:// to indicate the protocol to be used. A series of diagrams showing the sequence of events is helpful in explaining the transaction. In the first instance the client sends out an HTTP request over the Internet using TCP/IP to the destination web server

(microsoft.com). The structure of an HTTP request should be explained here. The destination web server application receives the request and attempts to find the requested web page. The requested web page maybe situated in various locations, a directory on the web server computer or on another computer to which the web server has access. When the web server finds that the requested web page does not exist, it constructs an HTTP response with the appropriate status code. Again the answer should give an example of an HTTP response with initial status and subsequent header lines. The answer should conclude by explaining what the browser does with the HTTP response.

2. There are two distinct parts to this question: one dealing with web server hardware and the other with web server software. When developing the requirements specification for the hardware it is important to reflect on the level of traffic now and its potential growth. If the level of traffic is likely to increase, then the NIC should be robust enough to deal with it, i.e. it should be of sufficient bandwidth to cope with the projected level of traffic. The importance of the websites that will be hosted also needs to be considered. If the websites are important, then both the NIC and the server computer need to be fault tolerant to some extent. The answer should describe a desirable server specification and what components should be fault tolerant, e.g. the processor, hard disks, motherboard and the NIC. The issue of the speed of access should be considered and the implications for the type of hard disk. The second part of the answer should consider the functionality of the new web server program. If the web server program needs to be secure, then what security features does the web server software need? If the new web server is going to be used as an intranet, then the web server must support user authentication that should be tied to the college user-management systems. Other issues that should be considered when choosing a web server program are:

- Will the server be used as proxy server?

- Will it be important to monitor and log the requests made?

- If the server is going to be used for dynamic content, what application environments does the server software support? Will the server software enable the web master to control what kinds of activities are permissible – e.g. executing a file?

- If the website content is complex and stored on various other servers, does the website software support virtual servers and aliases?

3.10: Further reading and research

Websites

Add the number in square brackets to **www.bookref.net/lpwm** for the most up to date web link, for example www.bookref.net/lpwm0110

www.w3.org/Protocols/rfc2616/rfc2616.html – details of HTTP 1.1. can be found on the World Wide Web Consortium site. **[0301]**

www.apache.org – details of Apache and downloads can be found from the Apache Foundation website. **[0302]**

http://news.netcraft.com/archives/2003/12/02/december_2003_web_server_survey.html – the Netcraft site contains lots of data and statistics on web servers and websites. **[0303]**

www.seoconsultants.com/tools/compression.asp – a site where you can check if your website is compression content. **[0304]**

www.webtechniques.com/archives/1998/05/engelschall/ – this site details how implementing a network of web servers can improve performance. **[0305]**

www.seoconsultants.com/articles/1000/server-performance.asp – this site provides details on a range of measures to implement to improve server performance. **[0306]**

www.serverwatch.com/tutorials/article.php/3436911/ – this site provides details on how to improve the performance of the Apache web server. **[0307]**

Books

Castro, E. (1999) *HTML 4 for the World Wide Web, Fourth Edition: Visual QuickStart Guide*, Peach Pit Press.

Musciano, C. and Kennedy, B. (2002) *HTML and XHTML: The Definitive Guide, 5th Edition*, O'Reilly and Associates, Inc.

Gandy, E and Stobart, G. (2005) *JavaScript: Creating Dynamic Web Pages*, Lexden Publishing: Colchester.

Irvine, P. (2005) *Computer Networks 2nd Edition*, Lexden Publishing: Colchester.

Chapter 4

NETWORK AND CONNECTION CONSIDERATIONS

Chapter overview

The way in which your website is made available over the Internet will affect how quickly users see your pages download. This chapter briefly looks at how the Internet and web are structured and work, then it examines how websites are hosted and any associated performance issues. This chapter also looks what intranets are and what are their associated performance issues.

Learning outcomes

After studying this chapter and answering the example questions and the end of the chapter (*see page 73*) you should aim to achieve these outcomes:

Outcome 1: Review the infrastructure of the Internet and the web.

Outcome 2: Appraise the options for hosting a website.

Outcome 3: List the performance issues of websites running on intranets and the web.

How will you be assessed on this?

You must understand how and be able to make your websites available over the Internet or on an organisational network. You should know the decisions that you need to make about hosting a site and any performance considerations. This chapter is likely to be assessed as an examination question or as part of an assignment where you are asked to outline the issues that need to be considered. Perhaps you might be given a scenario of 'a small five-man business' or 'a large corporation' on which to base your answers. Web hosting generally costs money, so you are unlikely to be asked to implement a fully-hosted website.

4.1: How the Internet works

You should be familiar with the idea of a computer-based network where two or more computers are connected together so that they can share resources, such as printers, and exchange information and files . A network that is limited to a room, building or site is called a **Local Area Network (LAN)** and when the geographic scale of the network grows beyond a few buildings to more than a few square kilometres it becomes a **Wide Area Network (WAN)** and involves different technology to LAN technology. To operate, networks need two essential elements:

- the medium or carrier by which computers are connected together, e.g. copper wire, fibre optic cable or microwave; and

- an agreed set of **protocols** that govern how a network should be used by the computers and devices connected to it, e.g. which device should use the network next.

Typically, a protocol determines:

- the naming convention for every device on the network;

- the system for agreeing which device should use the network at a particular moment;

- how information/data is transferred between devices; and

- the form in which information/data is transferred.

Protocols are embedded in the network hardware and software.

The Internet is a hierarchy of connected networks made up of LANs and WANs, just like the road system of a country is made up of private driveways, lanes, minor, major and trunk roads and then motorways. The 'motorways' of the Internet are the high speed **backbone** networks that are at least nation wide in size and generally constructed from bundles of fibre optic cable capable of transmitting up to 2.4 Gigabits of data per second. Backbones are provided by government departments and large corporations such as telecommunication companies. Backbones are connected together at **Network Access Points**, which are physical buildings where the backbone providers co-locate their network equipment to connect to each other. Next down in the hierarchy are the **Internet Service Provider (ISP)** networks that connect to an Internet backbone at a **Point of Presence**, which are the physical buildings in which the ISPs place their network equipment to connect to their chosen backbone. Sometimes backbone providers can be ISPs as well, such as British Telecom (BT), and sometimes small ISPs rent network capacity from larger ISPs. *Figure 4.1* illustrates the hierarchical structure of the Internet where IP packets travel up through from a client computer in a business at ➊ and its ISP ➋, up to the large ISP ➌ and its backbone provider ➍, then across to another backbone provider at a Network Access Point ➎ and down through to the destination web server at ➏.

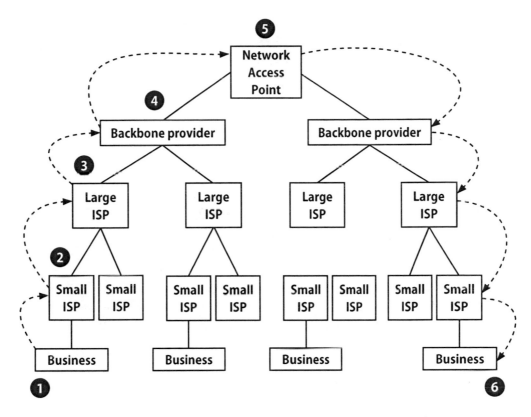

Figure 4.1: The hierarchical structure of the Internet

The Internet uses a particular set of **protocols** called the **Internet Protocol Suite (or Stack)**. The Internet Protocol Suite consists of several protocols, but the two most important ones are **Transmission Control Protocol (TCP)** and the **Internet Protocol (IP)**. Therefore, the Internet Protocol Suite usually is referred to by these two protocols as **TCP/IP**. TCP and IP work together to control and then transfer data and documents across the Internet. For example, when a web browser running on a **client** computer requests a web page from a web server somewhere on the Internet:

1. the TCP/IP software running on the web server will break the web page document up into smaller chunks of data or **packets** and label them in the correct order;

2. the TCP/IP then ensures that each packet has the destination address attached; and

3. the TCP/IP software running on the client computer will reassemble the packages in the right order based on the extra information attached to each packet.

The Internet Protocol part of TCP/IP requires that every device or computer on the Internet has a unique address – its **IP address**. Each IP address is made up of four numbers as shown in this example:

247.114.235.7

which is actually a shorthand way of representing the 32 digit binary address:

11110111011100101110101100000111

which when split into groups of eight bits or octets gives:

Binary:	11110111	01110010	11101011	00000111
Decimal equivalent:	247	114	235	7

The four octets incorporate two components: the net and the host. The net component is the organisation, e.g. a telecommunications company or ISP and the host is the specific computer in that net. There are three main classes of IP address as indicated in *Table 4.1 below*:

Class	Range	Use	Net component	Host component
A	1.0.0.0-126.255.255.255	Very large networks, e.g. backbone providers such as British Telecom	First octet – 62.	Last three octets – 134.44.183
B	128.0.0.0-191.255.255.255	Medium sized networks, e.g. the University of Wales	First two octets – 131.251.	Last two octets – 37.120
C	192.0.0.0-223.255.255.255	Small to medium sized businesses, e.g. Pembrokeshire College	First three octets – 194.83.91.	Last octet – 145

Table 4.1: Classes of IP address

How do the packets of data find their way from one computer to another over the Internet, e.g. from a web server to the computer that requested the page?

The answer involves devices called **routers** that maintain a list of the addresses of all the networks and computers connected to a **routing table**. Routers vary in size and sophistication from those that manage a simple network at home to those that manage connections to Internet backbones. *Figure 4.2* shows how routers fit into the Internet infrastructure.

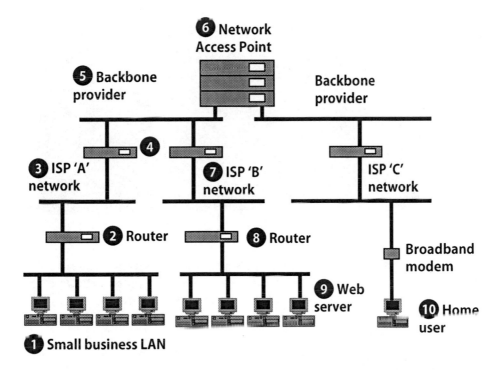

Figure 4.2: Illustration of the hierarchy of Internet routers

When the computer in the small business ❶ requests a web page from the web server hosted by ISP 'B' ❾, the local router ❷ checks its routing tables and works out that the request is not for any of the computers in its LAN and so forwards the request upwards to its ISP 'A' ❸. ISP A's router ❹ checks its routing table and realises that the web server is not known to it so it passes the request upwards to the backbone provider ❺. The address of the web server is within the backbone provider's range and the request is passed down via the routers at ❼ and ❽ to the correct web server. If the request for the web page had come from the home user at ❿ then the request would have had to jump from one backbone provider to another via the Network Access Point at ❻. The actual arrangement of routers in the Internet infrastructure is very much more complex than the illustration in *Figure 4.2* and the router at ❹ will be a much more powerful and sophisticated than the one at ❷.

You can check out the route of an IP packet from a source to destination computer and the routers it passes using the DOS **tracert** (short for trace route) command. If you are using a windows based computer, launch a DOS command prompt window and type in the tracert command followed by a URL as shown in the following example:

C:\> tracert www.bbc.co.uk

and you will get a similar output to this:

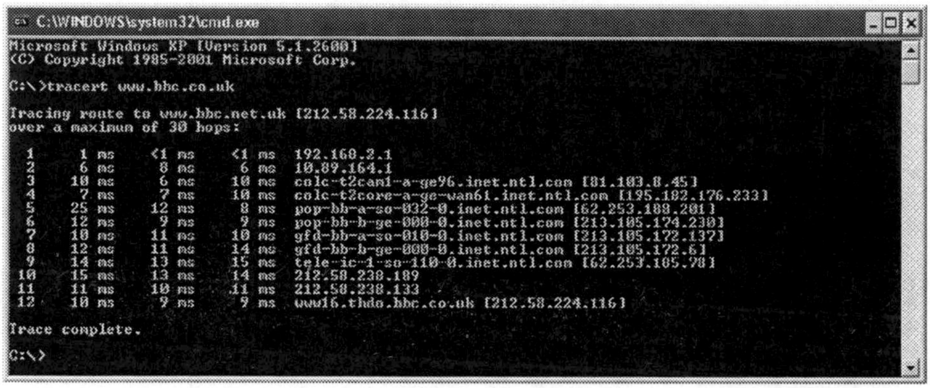

Figure 4.3: Tracert results

This shows all the routers that the IP packet passed through to get to the destination. Tracert measures the round trip time from source to router three times in milliseconds hence the three sets of figures in the above output. Notice at step 5 the packet reaches a class A address (first octet 62), which is the backbone provider BT.

> **TIP**
>
> For further information about the structure of Internet look at **http://navigators. com/isp.html** which contains very interesting material.

Even though the Internet is an amazing thing, it is only a network and does not do anything by itself. To be useful the Internet requires applications to make use of it, of which, e-mail and the World Wide Web are the most common, but there are many others. People often get the web and Internet confused, but it is important to distinguish between the two – the web is an application that uses the Internet. The operation of the web is described in detail in *Chapter 3, pages 35–52*.

The Domain Name System (DNS)

The four octets of the IP address give the world just short of 4.3 billion possible IP addresses, which is OK if you are a computer and can store addresses in a database, but humans are not so good at remembering long numbers. For this reason, the **domain name system** was introduced in 1984 to match up a human-readable **domain name** to an IP address so that people could use the domain name instead of the IP address.

You will be familiar with domain names when you browse to a particular website, such as:

www.bbc.co.uk   **www.google.com**   **froogle.google.com**

www.w3c.org   **validator.w3c.org**

The domain name is made up of three or four levels:

- There are several hundred of the first or top level domains (TLD) including **.com, .org, .edu, .net** and the two character country codes, e.g. **.uk** at the end of the domain name.

- To the left of the TLDs are the first-level sub domains, for example '.co' (indicating a company) and '.ac' (indicating that it is an academic organisation).

- To the left of the first level are millions of unique second-level domains. Examples of well known domains are 'google', 'w3c' and 'microsoft'.

- The left most bit of the domain name e.g. 'www' or 'froogle' in the examples above refer to the **host name**, i.e. the actual computer that hosts the website or Internet service, which means that there are a lot of computers on the Internet called 'www', but each associated with a unique domain name.

It is possible to have more than four levels in a domain name, but four is the norm

Figure 4.4 shows the first level **.uk** domain that has **.co, .ac** and **.org** as second level domains and underneath **.co** for instance are the third level domains, such as **Lexden** or **BBC**. To each third level domain is a host name, which is usually **www**, that by convention indicates that it is web server.

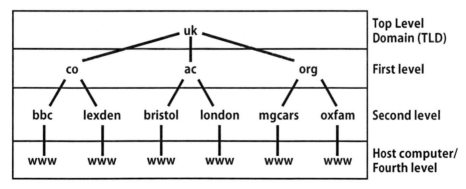

Figure 4.4: Structure of domain names

The IP address for the **www.bbc.co.uk** website is 212.58.224.82 so you could enter **http://212.58.224.82** in the address bar and it will take you to the BBC website. So how does your browser work out that www.bbc.co.uk is actually 212.59.224.82? The answer is a hierarchy of name servers, each with its own IP address and domain name, spread across the Internet that keep lists of IP addresses and associated domain names. When you type in www.bbc.co.uk

into the address bar your browser will ask its immediate name server if it knows the IP address for www.bbc.co.uk. Assuming that it does not know it will reply "I don't know the IP address of www.bbc.co.uk, but here is the IP address of a root name server that knows more than I do". There are 13 root name servers that keep lists of the several hundred name servers that handle the first level domains. So the root name server would say to your browser "here is a name server for the .uk domain". Your browser would then ask this root name server if it knows the IP address for www.bbc.co.uk. Assuming it does, it would return the IP address for the BBC website and it's only then that your browser is able to go to and retrieve the required web page. This process only takes a second or so and, for many websites, the process is much quicker because the various name servers along the way cache the records of IP addresses for which they have been asked. Note that there is no obvious correspondence between the four octets of the IP address and the levels of the domain name.

Management and the allocation of domain names

The **Internet Corporation for Assigned Names and Numbers (ICANN) (www. icann.org**) organisation handles the overall management and allocation of all domain names. ICANN is a non-profit corporation that has responsibility for IP address allocation, the top-level domains including the country codes plus the root server system management functions. ICANN was commissioned to perform these functions by the US Government. Other organisations can apply to ICANN to become an approved domain name **registrar** and there are many of them worldwide. ICANN publishes the details of all registrars on its **InterNIC** website (**www.internic.net**). The InterNIC site also includes the **WHOIS (www. internic.net/whois.html**) database that contains the details of the owners of all the top-level domains, excluding the country codes. ICANN has commissioned an organisation in each country to manage the domains for that country code. For example, in the UK, ICANN has commissioned Nominet (**www.nominet. org.uk**) to manage all the **.uk** domains and has its own WHOIS database.

If you want to register a domain, it is just a matter of visiting one of the name registrars for the top level domain that you are interested in, for example **www.easyspace.com** offers domain name registration; just fill out their online application forms and then complete an online transaction. This is explained in more detail in *Section 4.3, page 66*. When you register a domain with a particular registrar, your new domain name details will be stored on the registrar's name servers.

4.2:   Internet Service Providers (ISPs)

Most people will be familiar with the term **Internet Service Provider (ISP)**. The first ISP to offer dial-up connections to the Internet, The World (**www.theworld. com**), only started business in 1989 and the ISP industry has grown incredibly quickly since then. ISPs have been crucial in the dramatic expansion in the use of the Internet by offering their customers the ability to connect to the Internet easily. In this section, we consider ISPs in more detail.

The ISP industry is very competitive and includes small to very large companies. ISPs differentiate themselves by the variety and quality of services they offer and of course, the prices they charge. Some ISPs are nothing more than resellers for large ISPs as indicated in *Figure 4.1, page 55*. Some ISPs, such as BT, are large enough to be backbone providers themselves. Until a few years ago, most ISPs only offered connection via dial-up modems, but since then ISPs have been able to offer customers broadband connections to the Internet instead. Broadband connections now account for about 70% of all UK connections to the Internet[1].

Internet Service Provider technology

There are two main sets of technology employed by ISPs, dial-up and **asynchronous digital subscriber line (ADSL)**, i.e. broadband. *Figure 4.5* shows a typical arrangement for an ISP offering dial-up connection to the Internet to its clients.

In the first instance your computer will dial-up the ISP's access telephone number using it's modem **1**. The call will be answered by the ISP's **Remote Access Server (RAS) 2** which is just a specialised computer that can handle multiple telephone calls. The remote access server will establish a **Point to Point Protocol (PPP)** session with the connecting computer. The PPP session enables the connecting computer and the RAS to start exchanging data over an ordinary analogue phone line (note that this is not IP yet). The RAS obtains the connecting computers user id and password and queries the ISP's **Remote Access Dial In User Service (RADIUS)** server to check the details **3**. The RADIUS server maintains a database of all the ISP's users. The RAS will then issue the connecting computer with an IP address. Then, when the connecting computer requests a web page for example, the request passes via the RAS onto the ISP's internal network **8** and then one of the ISP's routers **4**. The router will be linked to the ISP's backbone provider **6** via a high speed connection (e.g. T1) with a device called a **Channel Service Unit/Data Service Unit (CSU/DSU)**, which is the equivalent of a 'high-powered' ordinary modem.

Figure 4.5: An ISP offering a dial-up service

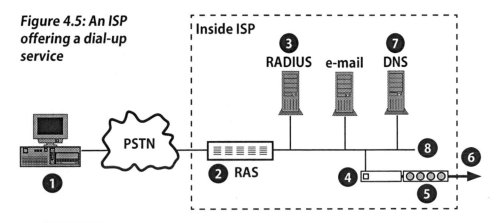

1 Source: **www.net4now.com/isp_news/news_article.asp?News_ID=3586**

> **NOTE**
>
> T1 is the data connection standard used in North America and Japan for transmitting data and voice and is capable of supporting speeds of 1.54 Mbps. In Europe, the E1 data connection standard is used and is capable of supporting speeds of 2.048 Mbps.

Figure 4.6 shows the more complex arrangement for an ISP offering an ADSL connection to its clients. The ISP element (dark grey) is the same as that in *Figure 4.5*. However, the link between the client computer and the ISP is more complex. With ADSL, the normal telephone signal is split into two components, the voice component and the data component (each component occupying different parts of the bandwidth) via a special **ADSL filter** ❶. When the telephone call connects to the exchange, the voice component is physically separated from the ADSL component and wired through to the PSTN. The ADSL component is wired through to the **Digital Subscriber Line Access Multiplexor (DSLAM)** ❸ that takes individual customer ADSL lines and bundles or multiplexes ❹ . These dedicated lines connect to one of BT's own RAS. When an ISP decides to offer ADSL it needs to enter into a contract with BT so that it can create accounts of the form 'username@ispname'. When a user connects to the Internet by ADSL, one of BT's RADIUS ❺ checks the account details against its database, and if this OK, a 'pipeline' is set up to the ISP via its own RAS ❻ and the customer account information for the ISP is checked by the ISP's own RADIUS. The link to the ISP's backbone provider is made in the same way as the dial-up arrangement in *Figure 4.6*.

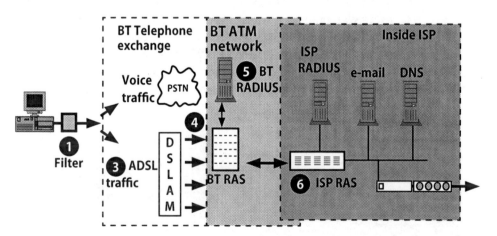

Figure 4.6: Making a broadband connection to the Internet

Choosing an ISP

ISPs differentiate themselves by the products, services and prices that they offer their customers, for example the amount of web space, the level and type of support. *Table 4.2* contains a list of the key aspects of the service offered by ISPs.

Connection type	Most ISPs offer dial-up and broadband at different levels of bandwidth, e.g. 1, 2 or 8 Megabits per second (Mbps).
E-mail	ISPs generally provide their customers with multiple e-mail accounts, that can usually be accessed through a web page interface or via a mail client such as Outlook Express.
Level of service	The level of service is a key factor in differentiating ISPs. Good ISPs should have clear terms and conditions and a code of practice. It is important to scan through these documents, which should be available on the ISP's website.
Web space	Many ISPs offer web space to their customers; this may vary from free web space with a URL generated by the ISP to fully-hosted websites using a customer's own domain. We consider the types of services that come with web space in *Section 4.3: Web Hosting, page 66.*
Support	ISPs generally offer some level of support to customers who may have questions or problems. The availability of support may be 24/7 or it may be limited to particular periods of the day. Support may be offered in a variety of ways including by telephone, e-mail, discussion boards or even instant messaging. ISPs may also have extensive interactive help files available online.
Value added services	ISPs may offer a variety of other services, including spam filtering, virus and spyware checking, parental control software, plus other miscellaneous products such as free telephone calls, static IP addresses and online data storage.

Table 4.2: Services that may be offered by ISPs

When choosing an ISP it is important to draw up a list of your requirements and rate a selection of ISPs against them. *Table 4.3* lists some of the key factors to consider. Several websites provide customer ratings of ISPs including, for example, **www.adslguide.org.uk**.

Fee	The cost of signing to an ISP varies between ISPs offering similar packages. It is therefore important to identify what value added services are included to distinguish the best ISP for you.
Metered/unmetered	Metering means charging for each period a customer is online. Periods might be in minutes or hours and vary depending on what time of day the service is used. You need to be able to calculate the likely cost of using an ISP, based on your patterns of use (e.g. two hours every evening). Metering generally only applies to dial-up services.
Customer service and technical support	How prompt is customer service/technical support and when do they guarantee to return your e-mail or phone call by? What is the quality of the support given and are they able to answer you questions satisfactorily? Is support free or does the ISP charge? What is the cost of using the support line, is it a free phone number?
Reliability	How often does the service become unavailable or 'flaky', i.e. does it fail frequently during the same session?
Speed	The speed of connection is difficult to judge because it depends on how far your home/business is from the local exchange in addition to any problems at the ISP or the carrier (e.g. BT) end.
Length of contract	The minimum length of contract that you need to sign up for will vary from ISP to ISP and some may charge for early cancellation.

Equipment included	Many ISPs will loan customers an ADSL modem within the contract and some contracts now include integrated routers that allow multiply computers to connect. Some routers supplied are also wireless-enabled and allow wireless devices such as laptops to connect.
Limits	You must check what limits are in place with the contract, e.g. maximum number of Megabytes per month data transfer or periods of the day/week when the service cannot be used.
Flexibility	Does the ISP require you to use its software to connect or access e-mail or does it allow you to use your own software? Does it require you to use its own type of browser?

Table 4.3: Factors to consider when choosing an ISP

Businesses have greater requirements of an ISP than domestic users since their connection will be shared between all its employees who need access to the Internet and e-mail. Business broadband requirements might include the following:

- higher bandwidth;
- increased reliability;
- a smaller **contention ratio**, which means fewer customers sharing the same dedicated line at ④ in *Figure 4.5, page 61*;
- static IP address for its domain;
- domain name and web hosting;
- increased/unlimited number of e-mail accounts; and
- larger storage capacity for e-mail messages.

ISPs generally offer separate services to business customers, but as businesses become larger, they will need to investigate other alternatives to ISPs, for example having their own dedicated high speed links to a backbone provider.

4.3: Web hosting

Websites must be hosted on web servers that are already connected to the Internet to make them visible on the web (*see Chapter 3, pages 35–52* for more details of how this is done). Most ISPs offer web hosting services, but so do many other online businesses. There are a large variety of options available when choosing a web hosting package and *Table 4.4*, below, lists the key options that are offered. It is important to draw up a list of your own requirements before making your choice.

Platform	The two main platforms are Microsoft Windows with Internet Information Server (IIS) or Unix with Apache (*see Section 3.6, page 46* for a comparison of the two platforms).
Web space	Web space is the amount of space in megabytes or gigabytes available for your site.
Bandwidth	The amount of data transfer allowed per period (usually a month).
Load balancing	Web hosting companies may have their network of servers configured so that high demands on particular sites can be shared amongst its servers to maintain the quality of service.
Programming/ scripting technology	Depending on server platform, you can choose (usually at extra cost) to use a variety of different programming languages to enhance your website, including ASP or ASP.NET predominantly on IIS servers and PHP or Perl predominantly on Apache servers. Many people use Microsoft FrontPage to build small-scale websites, but this requires a special 'add-on' to an IIS server.
Database technology	Customers who need to create dynamic websites will need to have access to a database management system on their web server. Again, depending on the platform, this will most often be Microsoft SQL server on IIS servers or MySQL on Apache servers, very small-scale websites might use Microsoft Access.
Media streaming	Some websites need to make audio or video clips available to visitors. For longer clips, it is advisable to employ a media-streaming server to handle the quantity of data that needs to be sent rather than downloading the whole file in one go.

File Transfer Protocol (FTP) support	To upload your web pages onto the hosting company's web servers you generally need to use a File Transfer Protocol (FTP) client. Some hosting companies have special web-based applications for uploading files instead of or in addition to FTP.
Forms support	Some companies offer web forms that can be customised to capture any required customer/visitor information.
E-commerce	Many hosting companies also offer their customers e-commerce facilities including a shopping basket and checkout system. To find out more about e-commerce, *see Chapter 10, pages 157–168.*
Visitor statistics	Hosting companies should offer customers visitor statistics and tools to analyse how many people visited the site during particular periods, etc.
SSL	If you need to ensure that transactions between the web server and the visitor are secure you can use the Secure Socket Layer (HTTPS) instead of the normal HTTP. To find out more about the SSL, *see page 44.*

Table 4.4: Key options when choosing a web hosting company

In addition to comparing the service features that hosting companies offer, it is also important to compare the quality of the service offered. *Table 4.5* lists some of the characteristics of the service that you should consider:

Performance	How reliable is the service, what guarantees on up-time are there? How often is data backed-up?
Customer support	What periods is customer support available? Is it for limited periods per day or 24/7? How many ways are there for customers to get support, e.g. e-mail, phone, forums or instant messaging?
Technical support	In addition to the question of its availability, how knowledgeable and helpful are the technical support staff?
Additional services	What other services does the web hosting company offer, for example instant notification when there is a problem via SMS or e-mail. Check there is adherence to quality standards such as 'Hosting Assured' (*see* **www.hostingassured.com**), Independent monitoring of up-time such as **www.alertra.com**, etc.

Table 4.5: Features of web hosting companies

The majority of web hosting packages are based on sharing multiple websites on the same server. However, if you are a web design company and wish to manage multiple sites, you can pay extra to rent a dedicated web server from larger hosting companies. Alternatively, you can pay the hosting company to look after your own server equipment at their data centres; a service called **colocation**.

You can roughly calculate the amount of storage capacity for your website based on the following formula:

Required capacity in Megabytes = Page size in Kilobytes * number of pages/1000

For websites with few images, the average page size is about 40 Kilobytes, but for sites with a great number of images, it is 70 Kilobytes. For example:

Required capacity in Megabytes = 70*120/1000 = 8 Megabytes

If you intend to add audio or video clips or other large files then you must calculate for these separately.

To calculate the approximate monthly bandwidth required use the following formula:

Required bandwidth (in Gigabytes) = (page size * number of pages viewed per visit * visitors per day * 31) / 1,000,000

The figure of '31' is the number of days in a month. A typical example might be:

Required bandwidth = (70 * 4 * 120 *31) /1,000,000 = 1.04 Gigabytes

In this instance, you might decide on a 2 Gigabyte per month package to be on the safe side.

Domain name registration

Having decided on an ISP and web hosting company (possibly the same organisation) you will need to register a domain name. As described earlier in this chapter, responsibility for maintaining records of registrations has been delegated to various agencies around the world called registrars. Easyspace. com is a typical registrar that now provides a range of extra services including web hosting. Domain name registration usually starts with a search to see if the domain you want is available. *Figure 4.7* shows the Easyspace search form.

Figure 4.7: The www.easyspace.com domain search form

Domain Name	Length of Registration	Cost*	Buy
www.gloop-it.com	2 Years	£24.00	✓
www.gloop-it.co.uk	2 Years	£9.50	☐
www.gloop-it.net	2 Years	£24.00	☐
www.gloop-it.org	2 Years	£24.00	☐

Figure 4.8: Choice of available domains

You enter the domain you want, choose the extension and then click the 'Search' button. If the domain you want is not indicated as having been registered by someone else you can then go on and purchase it using the online shopping system. You can, normally, only purchase a .co.uk domain for two years at a time, but others can be purchased for up to ten years. When you make the purchase, you will need to provide owner information that is passed onto the organisation responsible for maintaining the details for that top-level domain, which for the .uk domain is Nominet. Domain registrars offer a range of other services when you register a domain, some of which are free and some for which you have to pay for including all the various web hosting options already mentioned. *Table 4.6* lists the main services offered by domain registrars:

Name servers	Each domain registered must have at least two name servers so that when someone uses the domain in an e-mail or web address the request can be directed across the Internet to a specific server that can deal with it, even if it is only to say that 'the domain has be registered, but is dormant'.
E-mail forwarding	Once you have a domain, most registrars will offer e-mail forwarding, which means, for example, if someone sends an e-mail to geoff@gloop-it.com, it will be forwarded by the registrars servers to another identified e-mail address.
Web forwarding	Web forwarding is similar to e-mail forwarding in that if someone types in www.gloop-it.com in a browser, the registrars redirect the request to another web server. This is very useful if you have free web space with your ISP and do not wish to pay for full web hosting. You can redirect requests for www.gloop-it.com to your free web space. Registrars often offer free web forwarding, but usually this means that it will add banner adverts and the URL in the address bar will change to that of the free web space. Forwarding might be **cloaked**, which means the URL in the address bar remains the same with no banner adverts.
Subdomains	Some registrars offer customers the ability to create subdomains. The default domain is 'www', but you can add others, for example 'home' to create a new URL – home.gloop-it.com rather than www.gloop-it.com and then forward this URL to somewhere else.

Table 4.6: Services offered by domain registrars

There are many registrars and their prices vary, and therefore it is worth comparing their services. There are several websites that offer registrar comparisons (e.g. free versus paid-for web forwarding) and a good example is **www.regselect.com**. If you intend to become a web design company and will be registering and managing multiple domains, it is worth looking for a registrar who best supports that need, for instance, those that have well-designed online tools for making multiple registrations and managing domains.

4.4: Intranets and extranets

The generally held view is that **intranets** are networks restricted to use by a limited number of users (usually a single organisation) and based on using TCP/IP just the same as a mini Internet. Often intranets are nothing more than internal websites, but they can support a range of cross-organisation applications such as management information systems. There are several ways to prevent anyone from outside accessing an organisation's intranet. The two most common ways to create an intranet is to either use **private IP** addresses or a use a **firewall** or a combination of both. The **Internet Assigned Numbers Authority (IANA)** is the organisation commissioned by ICANN to coordinate global IP address allocation. The IANA has reserved three ranges of IP addresses for private use or within an organisation or home and these are:

Classes	From	To	Number of addresses
'A'	10.0.0.0	10.255.255.255	16,581,375
'B'	172.16.0.0	172.31.255.255	1,040,400
'C'	192.168.0.0	192.168.255.255	65,025

Any organisation can use these addresses internally for whatever purpose it chooses, but any device or computer that uses one must not connect to the Internet directly. So routers have to be configured not to forward requests from devices or computers with private IP addresses directly to the Internet. Since the IP addresses are private, computers outside of the organisation cannot communicate directly with computers and devices within the organisation. By using this approach, the organisation will establish an Intranet. Any web server in the Intranet must also have a private IP address.

A firewall is another way of controlling access from outside to computers inside an organisation, particularly malicious access from hackers. Firewalls are generally specialised computers or routers that are placed between the organisation and all its connections to the Internet. Firewall-computers enable people to implement security rules or **filters** to define which traffic can come in and which traffic can go out. The filters specify what happens to all requests from particular ranges of IP addresses, domains or protocols (e.g. HTTP, or FTP). Filters can block, or pass particular requests to all or specific computers or devices, e.g. 'all FTP requests go the organisation's FTP server, but all FTP requests to any other computer will be blocked'. Most domestic routers have inbuilt firewalls and *Figure 4.9* shows a typical set of firewall rules held by a domestic router. Therefore, it is possible to create an intranet using a firewall with specific rules that block external access and other rules that direct all internal IP traffic.

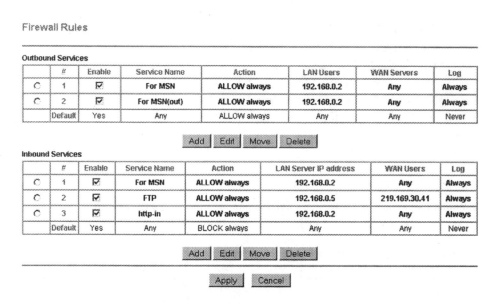

Firewall Rules

Outbound Services

	#	Enable	Service Name	Action	LAN Users	WAN Servers	Log
○	1	☑	For MSN	ALLOW always	192.168.0.2	Any	Always
○	2	☑	For MSN(out)	ALLOW always	192.168.0.2	Any	Always
	Default	Yes	Any	ALLOW always	Any	Any	Never

Add | Edit | Move | Delete

Inbound Services

	#	Enable	Service Name	Action	LAN Server IP address	WAN Users	Log
○	1	☑	For MSN	ALLOW always	192.168.0.2	Any	Always
○	2	☑	FTP	ALLOW always	192.168.0.5	219.169.30.41	Always
○	3	☑	http-in	ALLOW always	192.168.0.2	Any	Always
	Default	Yes	Any	BLOCK always	Any	Any	Never

Add | Edit | Move | Delete

Apply | Cancel

Figure 4.9: Firewall rules for a home router

Sometimes, some of the internal applications and resources of an intranet are made available to outside organisations, for example suppliers to a large business might need access to stock information on the intranet of another business. This arrangement is called an **extranet** and can easily be implemented using specific firewall rules that allow only certain domains access to the intranet.

4.5: Chapter summary

The Internet and web rely on particular protocols to function, especially TCP/IP, and all computers or devices connected to the Internet must have a unique IP address (or appear as if they do). Specialised computers, called routers, direct traffic on the Internet and around the web from simple home routers through to large complex ones that manage the Internet backbone. IP addresses are not easy for most people to remember so the Domain Name System maps them to names that can be easily understood. Domain name registrations are handled by a set of designated organisations in each country to ensure all domain names are unique.

Unless you are a very large organisation with its own WAN, individuals and smaller companies, need to contract with an ISP for their connection to the Internet. ISPs offer a varying range and levels of service so it is important to draw up a list of requirements against which to judge a selected few. Likewise with web hosting, you need to draw up a list of requirements before choosing a hosting company for your website. Intranets and extranets are IP-based networks running websites and other applications for a restricted group of people usually within one organisation. Many Intranets are implemented either using private IP addresses or firewalls, or a combination of both.

4.6: Example questions

1. What is the purpose of the Domain Name System and how does it operate?

2. How is traffic directed around the Internet?

3. If a small printing business with four employees, two of whom are office-based, has asked you to set up an e-mail account for the business, what steps do you need to take? Assume that the business does not subscribe to any Internet services at the moment.

4. The same printing business wants to set up a website to advertise its services in the first instance, but may be interested in selling its services via the website in the future. What factors would you take into account when choosing a website hosting company?

4.7: Example answers

The first two questions are likely form the first part of multipart examination questions and are designed to demonstrate your understanding of the underpinning technology. The second two questions above are likely to be latter parts of exam questions and are designed to demonstrate your ability to apply the underpinning knowledge in practice.

1. The answer to this question is straightforward: you would need to briefly explain IP addresses and their importance to the Internet and then the problem of remembering them. You can then explain how domain names were invented to make it easier for people to remember them. You would then need to go on and explain the structure of Domain Name System across the Internet, and finally, you might want to mention how the responsibility for maintaining the register of domains is managed by designated organisations in each country – registrars.

2. This question is simply asking you to explain TCP/IP and the structure of the networks that make up the Internet. You need to start by explaining that the Internet is a network of networks and each device or computer must have a unique address – IP address. You might want to explain the structure of an IP address. Then explain that for transmitting data the key Internet Protocols are TCP and IP. Explain the hierarchy of networks from private LANs to ISPs and then to the backbone providers. You might want to use an example of someone browsing a web page and the passage of that request across the Internet.

3. This question is asking you about selecting an ISP and the relevant services. You should start by working out the company's basic needs:

    i)   one or two e-mail addresses linked to a specific domain; and

    ii) a connection to the Internet.

    The first step is to draw up a list of requirements. You should be able to discuss the factors outlined in *Tables 4.2* and *4.3* – fee, metering, support, reliability, speed, length of contract, equipment included, limits and flexibility. A printing company is probably going to require quite a bit of bandwidth if it is going to send and receive image files, etc. The company must select an ISP provider that can offer it a relatively high bandwidth service. In addition, the reliability of the service will be critical since the business will be sending and receiving files from its customers.

4. This question is linked to the previous question. If the business wants a domain and e-mail address, it will probably want a website as well. It seems that the printing business only wants the website for advertising its services, therefore this tells you that the site will not be that big or complex. Again you must start by working out the company's requirements, perhaps by roughly estimating the amount of space and bandwidth it might need using the formulae on *page 68*. Then review each of the options offered by web hosting companies as listed in *Table 4.4, page 66*. The platform is not likely to be important since the web space requirements will be quite small. However, the company will probably want to have images to show the variety of work it does. If it's a small business, the level of traffic is likely to be quite low and will not need load balancing. The site is likely to be static so it won't need to subscribe to programming or database technology from its hosting company. There is a possibility that the company may want media streaming of video clips to show the workings of its business. The company will need FTP support to upload to its site and probably support for forms to gather inquiries. At this stage, the company will not need e-commerce, but would like to in the future, so the web hosting company should be able to offer this service. Visitor statistics will be important, but it is unlikely it will need SSL. You will then need to finish by outlining the importance of the characteristics listed in *Table 4.5, page 67*.

4.8: Further reading and research

Websites
Add the number in square brackets to **www.bookref.net/lpwm** for the most up to date web link, for example www.bookref.net/lpwm0110

www.icann.org – the Internet Corporation for Assigned Names and Numbers. **[0401]**

www.internic.net – list of all registrars maintained by ICANN. **[0402]**

www.nic.uk – Nominet, the registrar responsible for the .uk domain. **[0403]**

Chapter 5

WEB SERVER PROGRAMMING

Chapter overview

This chapter provides an overview of the technologies used to provide dynamic web pages to users. Server-side programming includes many different technologies so only a limited coverage is given here. If you are interested in knowing more about any particular technology mentioned here please refer to *Further reading and research, page 92*.

Learning outcomes

After studying this chapter and answering the example questions at the end of the chapter you should be able to achieve these outcomes:

Outcome 1: Outline the main server-side technologies.

Outcome 2: Choose an appropriate server-side technology for a website.

How will you be assessed on this?

It is likely that the content of this chapter is backed up by practical work in writing some server-side scripts or programs in a common language such as ASP.NET or PHP. The example questions at the end of this chapter (*see page 91*) are the typical of the type of questions that may be asked in an exam. In coursework you would be asked to explain your decisions in choosing a particular programming language or framework to complete a task. You might also be asked to write a report on the ways in which web pages can be made dynamic.

5.1: Server-side programming

In this section, we introduce the concept of server-side programming before covering each server-side programming technology and distinguish it from client-side programming.

Standard HTML pages are static, i.e. they are transmitted from the web server to the client as they are. It is often the case, however, that the content needs to be dynamic, i.e. it changes over time or because of parameters sent from the client. Examples of dynamic content include timetable information, online shops, search engines, online calendars, library catalogues and discussion boards. Web server software needs to be able to execute or pass control to third party programs to generate the dynamic content, i.e. **server-side programs** or **scripts**. In addition, the client browser may need to send data, such as a search string for a shop item, to a server-side program to generate the dynamic content. When dynamic content is requested by a client browser, the web server itself must execute the requested program or transfer control to the program. The dynamic output from the program is then passed back to the web server . The web server software then compiles the HTTP response containing the dynamic content and outputs it to the client browser. There are several standard technologies available that support this process and these are covered in this chapter.

An important aspect of server-side programming are the **environment variables**. These contain information about the client computer and the server computer that server-side programs can access, for instance it is sometimes useful to know which browser type the client computer is running so that the HTTP response can be made more appropriate for that browser. There are 20 or so standard environment variables and some servers define their own as well. Each server-side programming language implements a means by which it can read the environment variables and the *Section 5.2, page 78* shows how DATE_LOCAL is used. *Table 5.1* shows a list of the most common environment variables.

Environment variable	Value
HTTP_REFERER	The URL of the web page that called the server-side program or script.
REMOTE_ADDR	The IP address of the client computer.
HTTP_USER_AGENT	The browser type used by the client computer.
HTTP_COOKIE	The client computer's cookie, if one is set.
REQUEST_METHOD	Either set to GET or POST, the method for sending the query string (*see section 3.2, page 37* for an explanation).
QUERY_STRING	The query string (*see below* for an explanation).
ALL_RAW	The HTTP header set by a client computer.
DATE_LOCAL	The date and time at the web server.

Table 5.1: The most common HTTP environment variables

Passing data between a browser and the server

HTTP implements two means of passing user information from the client computer to the server in a HTTP request, the **GET** and **POST** methods. User information is usually obtained from a form in a web page (*see Section 6.2, page 96* for details). The GET method of a HTTP request appends the user information to the URL as a query string as shown in this example:

http://www.awebsite.com?firstname=bill&age=30

The query string is delimited from the URL by the '?' character and the query string consists of a number of 'name and value' pairs separated by the '&' character. The GET method limits the amount of user data that can be sent to about 2,000 characters since this is the maximum size that a URL can be. If information other than alphanumeric data or data greater than 2,000 characters is being sent, then the POST method should be used. The POST method causes a 'POST request' to be sent from the browser with the data included in the HTTP header not the URL. *Section 6.2, page 96* explains the use of POST and GET further when considering web forms and database queries.

5.2:   Server-side directives and includes

Server-side directives and, in particular, **includes** is a technique for rationalising the development of websites by enabling the development of a library of shared web page programs and scripts. This section shows how they work and how 'includes' can be used to rationalise website development.

Although server-side includes do not produce dynamic content they can be very useful in supporting it. These special directives instruct the server to do something extra, for instance inserting a 'time/date stamp' into the HTML file before the HTML file is sent to client browser. A server-side include file is just an ordinary HTML file, but with the directives added. A typical server-side directive to insert the server date and time would look like this:

```
<!--#echo var="DATE_LOCAL"-->
```

which would result in the HTML document containing the following line sent to the browser client:

```
Wednesday May 30 2007
```

Additional HTML code can be added to format the directive output so:

```
<b><!--#echo var="DATE_LOCAL"--></b>
```

will output the date and time in bold. *Table 5.2* contains a list of the server-side directives together with examples of their use.

Directive	Description
#FLASTMOD	Inserts the last time a file was modified.
#FSIZE	Inserts the size of a file.
#ECHO	Inserts the value of various environment variables.
#CONFIG	Configures how variables and commands are displayed.
#EXEC	Executes CGI scripts and inserts output into an HTML document.

Table 5.2: List of server-side directives

A typical page with all these directives added is shown in *Figure 5.1(a)* with the resultant HTML page sent to the client browser in *5.1(b)*. The file referred to as 'include.txt' in *5.1(a)* contains just the string `<b>I am include.txt</b>` enclosed in parentheses and could contain any other HTML, and the CGI program testcgi.exe outputs the words 'I am CGI program testcgi.exe', but could also output more HTML. On Servers running Microsoft Internet Information Server (*see Section 3.3, page 39* for details on web server software) files that contain server-side includes may need the extension 'stm' rather than 'html' for the server to recognise them.

```
<!DOCTYPE html PUBLIC "-//W3C//DTD XHTML 1.0
Transitional//EN" "http://www.w3.org/TR/xhtml1/DTD/
xhtml1-transitional.dtd">
<html xmlns="http://www.w3.org/1999/xhtml">
<head>
<title>TEST.STM</title>
</head>
<body>
1   <!--#include file="include.txt"--><br />
2   <!--#flastmod file="include.txt"--><br />
3   <!--#fsize file="test.stm"--> bytes<br />
4   <!--#echo var="DOCUMENT_URI"--><br />
    <!--#config timefmt="%m/%d/%y %H:%M:%S"-->
5   <!--#echo var="DATE_LOCAL"--><br />
    <!--#config sizefmt="bytes"-->
6   <!--#fsize file="include.txt"--> bytes<br />
7   <!--#exec cgi="/scripts/testcgi.exe" -->
</body>
</html>
```

(a)

```
<!DOCTYPE html PUBLIC "-//W3C//DTD XHTML 1.0
Transitional//EN" "http://www.w3.org/TR/xhtml1/DTD/
xhtml1-transitional.dtd">
<html xmlns="http://www.w3.org/1999/xhtml">
<head>
<title>TEST.STM</title>
</HEAD>
<body>
1   <b>"I am include.txt"</b><br />
2   Sunday April 04 2007<br />
3   0 bytes<br />
4   /test.stm<br />
5   04/04/07 06:07:46<br />
6   20 bytes<br />
7   "I am cgi program testcgi.exe"
</body>
</html>
```

(b)

Figure 5.1: (a) is an HTML document containing server-side directives (b) the resultant HTML document sent to browser

The most useful directives to support dynamic programming are **#include** and **#exclude** as they enable other files containing scripts or programs to be included within an HTML page. The include directive enables web developers to rationalise the development of their websites so that commonly used or shared elements can be referred to rather than repeating the same HTML or scripts on each page. Examples of the use of the **#include** directive include adding a standard header and footer to each web page, the navigation bar or, perhaps, a feedback form on each web page.

5.3: The Common Gateway Interface

The oldest technology for supporting server-side programming/scripting is called the **Common Gateway Interface (CGI)**, which is still used today. However, it is less efficient than more current technologies. The CGI was developed by the National Center for Supercomputing Applications (NCSA) and defines the way in which a web server can pass information to a third-party program, enable that program to run, pass back the output and then to pass this onto the client browser. *Figure 5.2* shows how CGI works:

1 An HTTP request is made to the server; from a client browser; **2** the server determines whether to simply return the requested file (e.g. an HTML document) or to execute the file via CGI; **3** the server passes control to the appropriate program via the CGI together with all the environment variables. It is up to the CGI script or program to 'read' the environment variables and ascertain if there is any data sent with POST or GET as well. If the form used the GET method, the contents of the form will be in the query string, if the POST method is used, the contents will be embedded in the HTTP request header. The CGI program either reads the QUERY_STRING environment variable if the GET method was employed or uses the 'Standard In' (STDIN) function if the POST method was used; **4** the CGI program operates on the user information and produces an output **5**; the output is passed back to the web server via the CGI; and then **6** the server forwards the output to the user.

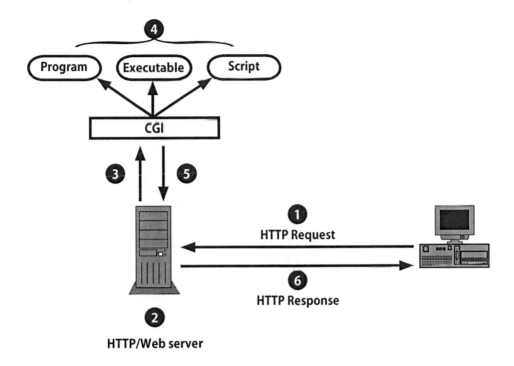

Figure 5.2: How the Common Gateway Interface operates

The CGI will work with any script or programming language; however, it has become more associated with a particular scripting language – **PERL**, especially on Apache-based servers. CGI scripts and executable programs have, in the past, been located in a directory called 'cgi-bin', which has permissions set to allow the scripts and programs to be executed, so a typical call to a CGI script might be:

http://www.anyweb.com/cgi-bin/env.pl

On IIS-based servers, any directory can act as a CGI directory by changing the permissions of the directory. The disadvantage of using CGI is that each CGI program must output a complete HTTP response with a fully-formed header plus the contents of the web page. The other disadvantage is that the web server must start a new process each time the same CGI program is called. This means that if the same script is called many times, then the server will slow down.

5.4: Server-side scripting with Active Server Pages

In this section, we consider the idea of scripts as a form of server-side programming.

Scripting is a form of programming where the code is interpreted line by line at run time rather than compiled as binary code. **JavaScript** is a scripting language commonly used in web pages that is executed by the client browser, but scripts can also be executed by the web server before being sent to the client browser, i.e. **Server-side scripting**. Scripts are embedded in a standard HTML page in the same way in which JavaScript is, but are executed by the server before the page is transmitted to the client browser. *Figure 5.3(a)* shows a simple example, the script begins with '<%' and ends with '%>' and sets the variable 'texttosend' to a string of HTML. Then the function response.write() outputs it to the browser. *Figure 5.3(b)* shows the resultant HTML; notice that the source script cannot be seen by the client browser.

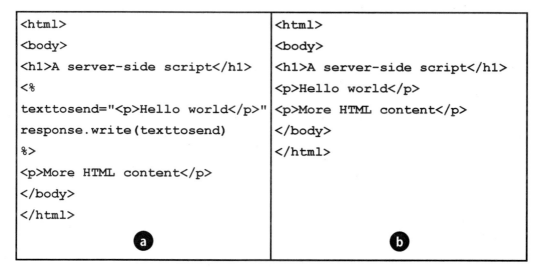

``html
<html>
<body>
<h1>A server-side script</h1>
<%
texttosend="<p>Hello world</p>"
response.write(texttosend)
%>
<p>More HTML content</p>
</body>
</html>
`` a
	``html
	<html>
	<body>
	<h1>A server-side script</h1>
	<p>Hello world</p>
	<p>More HTML content</p>
	</body>
	</html>
	`` b

Figure 5.3: (a) A simple example of a HTML document with a server-side script, (b) the results of the executed server-side script sent to the browser

In 1996, Microsoft introduced the **Internet Service Application Program Interface (ISAPI)**, which is a set of publicly-available functions that enable third-party applications to communicate directly with IIS. The first ISAPI application was called **Active Server Pages (ASP)**, a server-side programming technology designed to deal with the weaknesses of CGI. ASP uses **VBScript**, Microsoft's primary scripting language based on Visual Basic. ASP is an example of an **ISAPI filter**, which means that when a document with the extension **.asp** is requested from an IIS server it is the sent directly to the ASP filter, which is a dynamic link library file (dll) called **asp.dll**. The ASP filter parses the ASP file, executes any scripts it finds and returns the output directly to the client browser. *Figure 5.3* is an example of an ASP file.

ASP has a number of built-in **objects** to enable it to produce dynamic web pages. Objects in programming are self-contained packages of functions, constants and variables that can be used or manipulated for a common purpose. There are two important objects in ASP that enable it to obtain input from a user and client browser and send output back to the user. These are the **Request object** for getting information from a user and the **Response object** for sending information back to the user. *Figure 5.3* shows the 'write' function of the Response object used with the syntax '`response.write(any text string)`'. The Request object contains two elements that enable it to either retrieve data sent in a query string or via the Post method. If, for instance, the query string is :

http://www.awebsite.com?firstname=bill&age=30

the ASP code can retrieve the values of 'firstname' and 'age' with the lines:

```
Request.QueryString("firstname")
Request.QueryString("age")
```

To retrieve data sent with the post method assumes a web page form was used. To retrieve the same first name and age data that used the POST method would use the code:

```
Request.Form("firstname")
Request.Form("age")
```

TIP

To really understand ASP you need to create a few of your own ASP pages. Teaching ASP is outside the scope this book, but some of the references at the end of the chapter include tutorials showing you how to run ASP on your own computer. Also check out *Section 3.3, page 39* for details on how to install a web server on your computer.

5.5: ASP.NET

In 2000, Microsoft introduced their new strategy for Internet-based applications called **.NET** pronounced 'dot net'. .NET is Microsoft's strategy for all its next generation of Internet and Web-based applications. .NET includes a new framework for all Microsoft applications and is based around a shared set of components or services that use standards such as HTTP. The benefits of .NET will be greater efficiencies in application develop by using and reusing common services and more efficient applications. As part of this strategy, ASP, as described above, has been superseded by **ASP.NET**, which is different to, and not entirely compatible with, **classic ASP**. The problem with classic ASP is that the code and HTML are intermingled, making it very hard to write and difficult to understand. ASP.NET is different from classic ASP in that:

- the code is separated from HTML;

- it supports Visual Basic in full, not just VB Script;

- it supports **event driven programming**;

- it has improved performance since the code is compiled;

- more capabilities – programmable **controls** (e.g. buttons) and user authentication;

- it can be written in other programming languages such as C sharp and C++.

Any .NET code including ASP.NET is compiled into Microsoft Intermediate Language (MSIL) that is executed by the common language runtime (CLR) engine when the page is requested. The problem with this approach is that the first time an ASP.NET page is called, it takes longer to run, but then the page is cached for subsequent requests. *Figure 5.4(a)* shows how the ASP example in *Figure 5.3* would be written in ASP.NET and illustrates a number of important points about ASP.NET:

- all scripting is separated from the HTML (lines 1–7);

- in ASP.NET all output to be sent to the client browser must be included inside a **<form>** tag (line 10);

- the new attribute '**runat=server**' causes the server to execute the code before it is sent to the browser (line 10 and 12);

- ASP.NET introduces **event driven programming**. The function '**Page_Load**' only runs when the page is called for the first time. (line 2); and

- an ASP.NET label control called 'lb1' is used to output our message (line 12).

When the ASP.NET in *Figure 5.4(a)* is first called, the event **Page_Load** is triggered and it's associated subroutine (lines 2–6) is executed. The **Page_Load** routine declares the variable '**texttosend**' in line 3, assigns the value 'hello world' in line 4 and then sets the 'text' property of the 'label control' (line 12) to the value of the variable '**texttosend**'.

Figure 5.4(b) shows the output sent to the client browser; notice that inside the **<form>** tag there is an **<input>** tag (line 4) of type '**hidden**' called '__ VIEWSTATE' with a very long associated value. This hidden input tag means that any values held in the form are preserved when a user moves away and then returns to a page. This property of forms in ASP.NET is particularly useful in web applications, such as online shops, when a user is swapping from one page to another when completing a multipart form.

```
1   <script runat="server">
2   Sub Page_Load
3   Dim texttosend
4   texttosend="hello world"
5   lb1.text=texttosend
6   end sub
7   </script>
8   <html>
9   <body>
10  <form runat="server">
11  <h1>A server-side script</h1>
12  <p><asp:label id="lb1" runat="server"/></p>
13  <p>More HTML content</p>
14  </form>
15  </body>
16  </html>
```

(a)

```
1   <html>
2   <body>
3   <form name="_ctl0" method="post" action="test.aspx"
    id="_ctl0">
4   <input type="hidden" name="__VIEWSTATE" value="dDw5MjM
    zODA0MjI7dDw7bDxpPDE+ Oz47bDx0PDtsPGk8MT47Pjts8 =" />
5   <h1>A server-side script</h1>
6   <p><span id="lb1">hello world</span></p>
7   <p>More HTML content</p>
8   </form>
9   </body>
10  </html>
```

(b)

*Figure 5.4: (a) ASP.NET source code and
(b) ASP.NET browser output*

Controls are a key element of ASP.NET and each one has various **properties** that can be set. ASP.NET supports three types of control:

- **HTML Server Controls** – traditional HTML tags;
- **Web Server Controls** – new ASP.NET tags;
- **Validation Server Controls** – for input validation.

HTML controls are identified in ASP.NET by giving the HTML tag such as `<table>` an '`id`' and '`runat`' attribute as in the following line:

```
<table id="tab1" border="1" runat="server" />
```

Everything about the table can then be controlled by the ASP.NET code.

Web server controls and validation controls are completely new and provide extra capabilities not present in classic ASP. Web server controls and validation controls are identified in ASP.NET like so:

```
<asp:control_name id="some_id" runat="server" />
```

So a declaration of a label control as shown in line 12, *Figure 5.4(a)*, would be:

```
<asp:label id="lb1" runat="server"/>
```

Figure 5.4 shows how ASP.NET provides the equivalent of the classic ASP `Response.Write()` function. *Figure 5.5(a)* is the ASP.NET equivalent of the `Request.Form()` function. The form between lines 8 and 13 contains a server control textbox (line 10), a server control submit button (line 11) and a paragraph tag HTML control (line 12).

The HTML that is sent to the user is shown in *Figure 5.5(b)*; notice that when the form is sent, the ASP.NET compiler automatically makes the ASP.NET file the subject of the action, i.e. `action="inputtext.aspx`" (line 3).

```
1  <script runat="server">
2  Sub submit(sender As Object, e As EventArgs)
3    p1.InnerHtml = "<b>You wrote:</b> " & txt1.Value
4  End Sub
5  </script>
6  <html>
7  <body>
8  <form runat="server">
9  Enter some text:<br />
10 <asp:TextBox id="txt1" runat="server" />
11 <input type="submit" value="Submit"
   OnServerClick="submit" runat="server" />
12 <p id="p1" runat="server" />
13 </form>
14 </body>
15 </html>
```

(a)

```
1  <html>
2  <body>
3  <form name="_ctl0" method="post" action="inputtext.
   aspx" id="_ctl0">
4  <input type="hidden" name="__VIEWSTATE" value="dDwxN
   zA1MdkxNzQwOz=" />
5  Enter some text:<br />
6  <input name="txt1" type="text" id="txt1" />
7  <input name="_ctl1" type="submit" value="Submit" />
8  <p id="p1"></p>
9  </form>
10 </body>
11 </html>
```

(b)

*Figure 5.5: (a) ASP.NET source code and
(b) ASP.NET browser output*

5.6:   Cookies

HTTP is a stateless protocol, which means that when a web server has dispatched a web page or file to a browser it forgets everything about that browser and its user. However, in many instances, such as online shops, it is necessary for the web server to maintain information about the user such as the pages they have already visited, what items have been added to their basket, personal details and their preferences. In 1995, to support this need, the Netscape Communications Corporation developed the idea of a **cookie** – a small piece of textual information shared between a web server and browser. When a web server first sends a web page to a browser, it also sends a cookie with information about the user stored in it. When the user's browser next makes a request to that web server, the browser also sends the cookie that the web server reads and hence can send back user-specific pages back. A browser may store many cookies, each specific to a particular web server. A simple example of the use of a cookie would be personalising a web page with the name of the user who requested it.

There are some limitations to cookies:

- they can only store 4,096 bytes;

- most browsers set a limitation on the number of possible cookies, usually 20 per site; and

- browsers can be set to refuse cookies.

Any cookie can contain several **name and value pairs**, an expiry date and a path for example, so that the web server can associate different parts of a site with particular cookies.

Cookies enable a web server to maintain continuity with the browser and its user, i.e. the web server always knows what state the browser is in, what page has been requested and who requested it, i.e. **state management**. Here is a typical example of a cookie with a session ID and username name-value pairs:

```
details
SESSIONID=4578&USERNAME=Bill
localhost/test
1024
2983885312
29653678
2401143168
29647442
*
```

The ASP.NET Response object has a collection (i.e. a set of related functions and properties) named 'Cookies' for setting cookies and the Request object has a collection also named 'Cookies' for reading them. In this simple example, the Response object is used to set a cookie with the user's name:

```
Response.Cookies("username").Value="Bill"
```

In this example, the Request object is used to read the cookie called 'username' and assign it to an ASP.NET text label so that web pages can be tailored to include the user's name:

```
Label1.Text=Request.Cookies("username").Value
```

This section has only given a brief overview of cookies and how to set and read them. To find out more see the reference to the Microsoft Development Network at the end of this chapter on *page 92*.

5.7: Other programming languages

There are other programming languages that are used in server-side programming.

PHP

PHP (which stands for PHP Hypertext Preprocessor) is a programming environment that was developed for the Apache web server, but is now available for IIS. PHP's close association with Apache means that it inherits all the strengths of Apache, for instance its robust security. In keeping with Apache, PHP is open source, which means bugs are fixed rapidly, and has a large library of modules available to support various needs. Like ASP.NET, PHP is a scripting language and is compiled when a page is requested and then cached for future requests, making it faster than classic ASP, but probably not ASP.NET. If a website is based on an Apache server, it makes sense to use PHP rather than ASP or ASP.NET.

DID YOU KNOW?

. PHP is an example of a 'recursive acronym' – the term PHP includes itself, i.e. the 'P' in PHP stands for 'PHP' so:

'PHP Hypertext Preprocessor' expands to:

'PHP Hypertext Preprocessor Hypertext Preprocessor' that expands to:

'PHP Hypertext Preprocessor Hypertext Preprocessor Hypertext Preprocessor' and so on.

An example of programmers having fun!

Java

Sun Microsystems introduced a Java language-based server-side programming environment called **servlets**. Servlets are Java programs designed to run with a web server just like ASP.NET or PHP pages. Java is an **object oriented** programming language which means that it is should produce very efficient programs. Very crudely, 'object oriented' means blocks of code are 'bundled' up into objects or classes that can be used by other Java objects or classes. This means Java code can be reused much more efficiently and effectively than non-object orient languages. Java servlets are compiled into machine-independent code that is executed by the Java Virtual Machine when the servlet is requested. The Java Virtual Machine is a program that runs in the background. Since servlets are written in Java, the strengths associated with Java also relate to servlets, i.e. they are object oriented, so code used in one servlet can be used in others. The other advantage of servlets is that the code compiled into machine code runs very fast. Servlets have several in-built classes similar to ASP objects called 'response', 'request', 'session', and 'application' that allow programmers to develop server-side applications.

Java Server Pages (JSP)

In addition to servlets, Sun Microsystems also introduced **Java Server Pages (JSP)**, which are similar to PHP and ASP.NET in that the Java code is included in a web page and not compiled. However, when a request is made for JSP pages, the scripts they contain are dynamically translated into servlets and then executed. The benefit of using JSP pages is that programmers can develop Java applications in a scripting environment without the strictures of creating Java classes. JSPs also enable programmers to create their own HTML-like tags that can be reused elsewhere. Any tags developed are held in a tag library so that they can be used by all other JSP pages. One of the great advantages of servlets and JSP is that they are platform and web server independent so code written on one platform, for instance Microsoft Windows, will run on another platform such as MacIntosh.

5.8: Chapter summary

ASP.NET, PHP and JSP/servlets have their strengths and weaknesses and different developers will argue that one is faster or more efficient that another, but there are no definitive comparisons available so it is impossible to say which is best. The best comparison is, therefore, in terms of their features. ASP.NET is flexible in that code can be written in several languages whereas PHP and JSP/servlets are single languages. ASP.NET is highly object oriented and is part of the .NET framework so it can take advantage of all the other elements of .NET, making it a very powerful development environment. The disadvantage of ASP.NET is that it is entirely dependent on everything else being Microsoft-related products, hence limiting its application to Microsoft sites. Since ASP.NET is proprietary, developers are dependent on Microsoft for maintaining, updating and extending it.

PHP has a number of advantages – it is open source, there are many free resources, support is available from the PHP developers' community, who also rapidly fix any bugs. PHP is also available on IIS and Apache, but it has better associations with Apache.

The benefits of JSP/servlets are that they are platform independent and there are free tag libraries available for many different uses.

5.9: Example questions

1. How can web pages be made dynamic?

2. You are a web developer and you have been given a brief for a new website. The new website will be an online magazine to which people will subscribe, the magazine is broken down into sections and people are likely to focus on particular sections of the magazine only. The brief asks you to ensure the site is personalised. What decisions do you need to make and how will you enable the site to be personalised?

5.10: Example answers

1. This is a straightforward question that is trying to test what you know about the difference between static web pages and those that are created at the time they are requested, i.e. dynamic pages. You are likely to be familiar with at least one server-side programming or scripting language, which will help you to answer this question. If you have not learnt a server-side programming/scripting language, the contents of this chapter are enough to be able to answer it. Start by explaining what static web pages are, i.e. files containing HTML that are sent as they are to the client browser. Briefly explain why there is a need for dynamic web pages – personalised pages, discussion boards, online shops, etc. Then explain what server-side programming/scripting is, ideally with reference to a particular language – ASP.NET for instance. It is important to mention the request and response objects and how cookies can be used for state management purposes. If you are able to write down some example fragments of code to illustrate your answer, it will improve your answer. Excellent answers will also mention that dynamic pages can be created with client-side technology with tools such as JavaScript and Flash, although these are not covered in this book.

2. This question is giving you opportunity to say what you know about server-side programming/scripting in a structured way. The first decision is deciding which elements of the site should be personalised, e.g. will the site know the readers' names, which pages they have already visited, which are their favourite pages and will it tailor the way the layout of pages of the online magazine are arranged? Secondly, you need to decide how you will make the site dynamic. This means explaining the strengths and weaknesses of main server-side programming/scripting languages. You might also explain the use of cookies for state management purposes. It would be useful if you are able to demonstrate how the site can be made dynamic with some example code showing how cookies work and how the users' names can be placed on the page.

5.11: Further reading and research

Websites
Add the number in square brackets to **www.bookref.net/lpwm** for the most up to date web link, for example www.bookref.net/lpwm0110

Server-side includes:

www.bedrockcomputers.co.uk/bedrockcomputers/httpenv.html [0501]

for Apache
http://httpd.apache.org/docs/howto/ssi.html [0502]

for IIS
www.microsoft.com/windows2000/en/server/iis/default.asp?URL=/ windows2000/en/server/iis/htm/core/iisiref.htm [0503]

Microsoft .NET
http://msdn.microsoft.com/netframework/ [0504]

The Common Language Runtime (CLR)
www.theserverside.net/articles/showarticle.tss?id=DM_CLR [0505]

ASP.NET
www.asp.net/Default.aspx?tabindex=0&tabid=1 [0506]

http://samples.gotdotnet.com/quickstart/aspplus/doc/default.aspx [0507]

Cookies in ASP.NET can be found in the Microsoft Developer Network Library by searching for 'basics of cookies' or try the URL:

http://msdn.microsoft.com/library/en-us/dv_vstechart/html/ vbtchASPNETCookies101.asp [0508]

PHP
www.php.net [0509]

Servlets

http://java.sun.com/products/servlet/overview.html [0510]

Java Server Pages (JSP)
http://java.sun.com/products/jsp/overview.html [0511]

Chapter 6

DATABASES AND WEB SERVERS

Chapter overview

This chapter presents enough detail to enable you to understand the basics of how databases work and how they are used in conjunction with web servers to produce web pages It contains some example scripts to illustrate how web pages connect to databases.

Learning outcomes

After studying this chapter and answering the example questions at the end of the chapter (*see Section 6.5, page 106*) you be able to achieve these outcomes:

Outcome 1: Explain how databases are used to create web pages.

Outcome 2: Discuss the issues of using databases in website development

How will you be assessed on this?

In coursework, you would be expected to explain how websites work with databases and why. You might be given an example scenario and asked how the example could be made dynamic using a database. It is likely in some courses you would be expected to produce live examples of database-driven websites using a scripting or programming language that you have been taught. It is likely you will be receiving support to use a particular script or programming language.

6.1: Databases

This section introduces the main concepts in the design and structure of databases.

In *Section 5.1, page 76*, it was pointed out that it is often necessary for web pages to be dynamic, i.e. generated, on the fly, as they are requested and placing data, such as personal information, into it. Server-side programs or scripts are used to generate dynamic web pages, but any information required needs to be stored somewhere where the program can get a hold of it. This kind of information could be stored in text files, but usually it is stored in a database.

Databases are collections of related information stored together. A database consists of at least one **table** of data, as shown in *Figure 6.1*, where data is stored in rows or **records**. The column headings of a table in a database are referred to as **fields** or **attributes**. Each record in a table must be unique in some way, otherwise accessing the information would result in errors. To ensure that this is the case, at least one field must contain unique values for every record, for example a reference number. This field is called the **key**.

user_id	surname	name		
1	Elliott	Geoff		
2	Cunliffe	Daniel		
3	Jones	Bob		

Figure 6.1: A single table database

Generally, databases consist of many tables connected or 'related' to each other. They are related in that the key field from one table is included as a field of another as shown in *Figure 6.2*. This is called a **relation**. By inserting key fields from one table into another means it is possible to combine the information from both tables. *Figure 6.2* shows an example of a user's history of purchases from an online shop with three tables designed for storing information:

- the 'Users' table contains details of a registered user to the online store where the 'user_id' is the key;

- the 'Shopping_trolley' table contains details of each trolley created as users begin shopping; and

- the 'Trolley_contents' table contains the actual contents of the trolley.

Notice that the 'Shopping_trolley' table contains the 'user_id' field from the 'Users' table – this is the way that tables are connected. By connecting tables like this it is means it is possible to find the surname of the person who owns that shopping trolley by knowing the 'trolley_id' from the 'Shopping_trolley' table. For a full coverage of databases *see Further reading and research, page 107.*

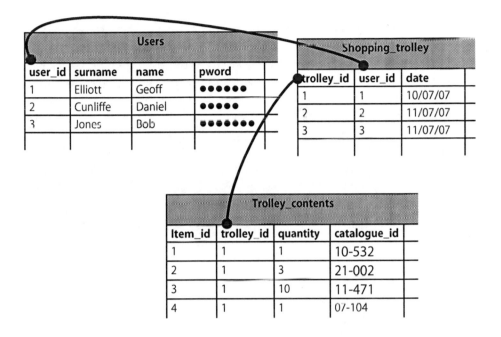

Figure 6.2: Three related tables in a database designed for use with an online shop

---

TIP

Lecturers prefer to use actual examples in their lectures and assessments rather than considering things in the abstract. Try to develop some worked examples of typical uses of databases in website design – an online shop, or a membership site. It is likely that they will ask a question about a similar kind of application.

6.2:   Web page forms

In this section we will consider the general principles of obtaining information from the user with web page forms.

Figure 6.3 illustrates a scenario whereby a user of an online shop wishes to view their account details. Here the user would need to access information in the appropriate database on the web server. To do this the first thing the user would be required to do is log onto the website in order to identify themselves. This would be done by completing a **web page form** with a user name and password and submitting the web form's contents to the web server using a submit button as shown in **❶**. Then the server either passes the contents onto another application or runs the script or program identified by the web page form **❷**. The script or program then reads the contents of the web page form, queries and compares the user name and password given with the records in the users table of the online store database **❸**. Assuming there is a positive match the script or program sends back a confirmation page to the user's browser **❹** via the web server and the user can gain access to their account details.

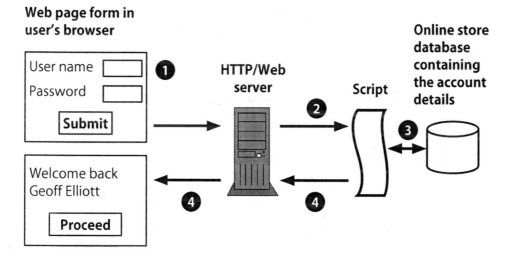

**Figure 6.3: The sequence of events when
a user submits a form to a web server**

TIP

The database may either be stored on the same computer as the web server or on a separate computer.

Web page forms enable data to be entered in several different ways as shown in *Figure 6.4.*

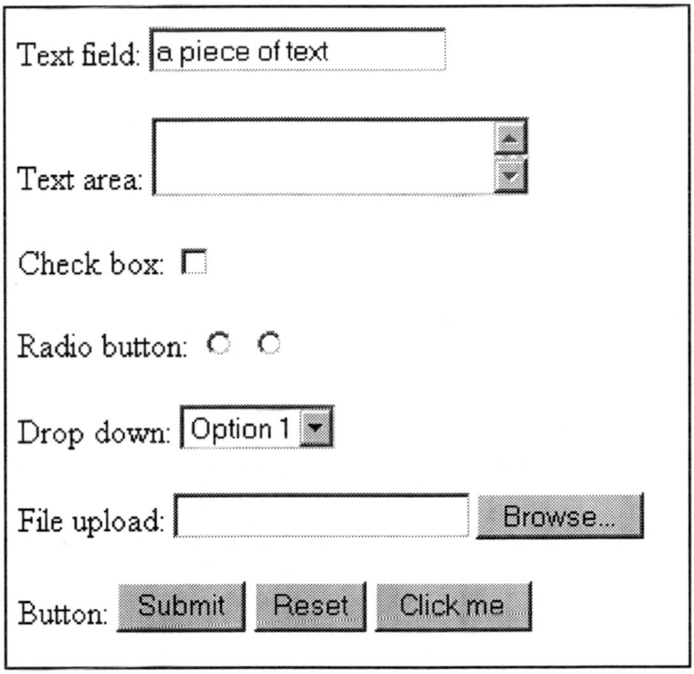

Figure 6.4: Web page form with various ways for entering data

Web page forms can be built in several different ways, either in static HTML, or with some server-side scripting. In ASP.NET, each type of input element can be constructed using predefined objects (*see Section 5.4, page 82* for an explanation of ASP objects). The HTML code required to build the form in *Figure 6.4* is shown in *Figure 6.5, page 98.* Each input tag has attributes to define its type, name and initial value.

```
  <form action="scrpt1.asp" method="post">
<br />
  Text field:
    <input type="text" name="textfield" value="a piece
of text">
<br />
Text area:
  <textarea name="textarea"></textarea>
<br />
    Check box:
      <input type="checkbox" name="checkbox"
 value="checkbox">
<br />
    Radio button:
      <input type="radio" name="radiobutton"
 value="yes">
  <input type="radio" name="radiobutton" value="no">
<br />
Drop down:
<select name="Drop down">
    <option>Option 1</option>
    <option>Option 2</option>
    <option>Option 3</option>
  </select>
<br />
File upload:
  <input type="file" name="file">
  <br />
Button:
    <input type="submit" name="Submit" value="Submit">
    <input type="reset" name="Reset" value="Reset">
    <input type="button" name="b1" value="Click me">
    </form>
```

**Figure 6.5: HTML code used to construct the web page
form shown in Figure 6.3**

Once a form has been completed, its contents need to be sent to an application
or script located on the web server. The **<form>** tag in *Figure 6.4.* has the
attributes **action** and **method**:

- the **action** attribute defines the URL of the program or script that will receive the contents of the form; and

- the **method** attribute defines how the data will be sent – either appended to the URL (GET) or included in the HTML header (POST).

(*See Section 5.1, page 76* for more on the GET and POST methods.)

Users send completed forms back to the web server by clicking a **submit button**, which is a form button of type 'submit'. When the user clicks the submit button the browser knows that it has to send an HTTP response to the server with the contents of the form. In the example in *Figure 6.5* the contents of the form are sent to the ASP script **scrpt1.asp** via the post method. There are two other types of button, a general button of type 'button' and one of type 'reset' that when clicked causes the contents of the form to be cleared.

The process of building web page forms in ASP.NET has been simplified from classic ASP because ASP.NET has in-built controls (*see Section 5.4, page 82*) for creating and processing forms. *Figure 6.6* shows how the example given in *Figure 6.4* would be represented in ASP.NET. The difference with an ASP.NET and a classic ASP form is that the contents of the form are sent back to the same script file, hence there is a subroutine for processing the contents of the form when it is submitted as shown in the following example:

- the button control in line 30 has the 'onClick' attribute that causes the subroutine called 'submit' (lines 2–8) to be executed;

- ASP.NET allows buttons other than the submit button, as is the case with the button in line 32 that causes the subroutine called 'clickme' (lines 9–11), to be executed;

- line 18 creates a text box;

- line 19 creates a multiline text box;

- line 20 a checkbox;

- lines 21–24 two paired radio buttons (i.e. you can only click one);

- lines 25–29 a drop down list; and

- line 31 a reset button to clear the form. In ASP.NET forms, the contents of the form are not automatically cleared when the page is submitted so a reset routine needs to be written to clear the contents. In this case the reset subroutine (lines 12–14) redirects the browser back to the form.

```
<!DOCTYPE html PUBLIC "-//W3C//DTD XHTML 1.0
   Transitional//EN" "http://www.w3.org/TR/xhtml1/DTD/
   xhtml1-transitional.dtd">
1  <script runat="server">
2  Sub submit(Source As Object, e As EventArgs)
3    tb1.Text= txtfd1.Text
4    tb2.Text= txtfd2.Text
5    tb3.Text= chckbx.checked
6    tb4.Text= rdbutlist.selecteditem.value
7    tb5.Text= drop1.Selecteditem.Text
8  End Sub
9  Sub clickme(Source As Object, e As CommandEventArgs)
10 'some code here
11 End Sub
12 Sub reset(Source As Object, e As CommandEventArgs)
13 response.redirect("form1.aspx")
14 End Sub
15 </script>
16 <html xmlns="http://www.w3.org/1999/xhtml"><body>
17 <form runat="server">
18 <asp:TextBox id="home" runat="server" />
19 <asp:TextBox id="textfield" Text=" a piece of text
   "TextMode="MultiLine" runat="server" />
20 <asp:CheckBox id="checkbox" Text="" runat="server" />
21 <asp:RadioButtonList id="radiobutton" runat="server">
22 <asp:ListItem>Item 1</asp:ListItem>
23 <asp:ListItem>Item 2</asp:ListItem>
24 </asp:RadioButtonList>
25 <asp:DropDownList id="drop1" runat="server">
26 <asp:ListItem>1 </asp:ListItem>
27 <asp:ListItem>2</asp:ListItem>
28 <asp:ListItem>3</asp:ListItem>
29 </asp:DropDownList>
30 <asp:Button id="button1" Text="Submit"
   OnClick="submit" runat="server" />
31 <input type="reset" value="reset" runat="server"
   OnClick="reset" runat="server" />
32 <asp:Button id="b1" Text="Click me"
   CommandName="someaction" OnCommand="clickme"
   runat="server"/>
```

```
33 <br />
34 You submitted the following:
35 <asp:label id="tb1" runat="server" />
36 <asp:label id="tb2" runat="server" /><br />
37 <asp:label id="tb3" runat="server" /><br />
38 <asp:label id="tb4" runat="server" /><br />
39 <asp:label id="tb5" runat="server" /><br />
40 </form>
41 </body></html>
```

Figure 6.6: A web page form created in ASP.NET

Typically, when a user submits a web page form, the associated script sends back another web page with the information that was submitted for confirmation of its accuracy. This is done with the submit routine (lines 2–8 *Figure 6.6*). This script sets the text of five text boxes (lines 32–36) to the information that was submitted.

When a user enters data into a form it is important that they enter the correct information. In order to ensure that this is so, designers usually build in **validation** routines to check the user's data before the form is sent. ASP.NET has special controls designed for handling validation as shown in the simple example in *Figure 6.7*. In this script:

- the user enters a number (lines 7–8);

- when the form is submitted (line 10) the rangevalidator control (lines 14–20) validates the data;

- in this case the value must be between 1 and 1000 (lines 16–17) and of type integer (line 18);

- if a value not between 1 and 1000 is entered, the message in line 20 is displayed; and

- the rangevalidator control produces JavaScript code that is embedded in the web page form sent to the browser. Hence the validation is all undertaken in the client's browser before the form is returned.

```
<!DOCTYPE html PUBLIC "-//W3C//DTD XHTML 1.0
   Transitional//EN" "http://www.w3.org/TR/xhtml1/DTD/
   xhtml1-transitional.dtd">
1  <script runat="server">
2  Sub submit(sender As Object, e As EventArgs)
   'some code here
3  End Sub
4  </script>

5  <html xmlns="http://www.w3.org/1999/xhtml"><body>
6  <form runat="server">
7  Enter a number from 1 to 100:
8  <asp:TextBox id="tb1" runat="server" />
9  <br /><br />
10 <asp:Button Text="Submit" OnClick="submit"
   runat="server" />
11 <br /><br />
12 <asp:Label id="lbl1" runat="server" />
13 <br />
14 <asp:RangeValidator
15 ControlToValidate="tb1"
16 MinimumValue="1"
17 MaximumValue="1000"
18 Type="Integer"
19 EnableClientScript="false"
20 Text="The value must be from 1 to 1000!"
   runat="server" />
21 </form></body></html>
```

Figure 6.7: An ASP.NET script showing a validation control (lines 14–20)

6.3: Reading from and writing to databases

The real power of websites is when they are combined with databases to dynamically generate content. In this section we explore how websites read and write to databases using simple examples in ASP.NET.

Databases are created using software applications called **database management systems (DBMSs)** that enable programmers to create databases, tables and fields and insert, amend and delete data. DBMSs use a language called **Structured Query Language (SQL)** that is used to create and manage its databases. There are several vendors of DBMSs, of which the most commonly used are Microsoft Access, Microsoft SQL server, Oracle, and MySQL. Unfortunately, they all have their own versions of SQL. Microsoft SQL server and

MySQL are the most commonly used for websites – SQL server on Windows-based web servers and generally MySQL on Unix based web servers. Server-side scripts use SQL to control databases managed by a DBMS.

When designing a new database-driven website the developer must consider the key issue of traffic volume to the site; if it is very small, then a database such as Microsoft Access will be sufficient. If the volume of traffic is high, then a more powerful DBMS, such as Microsoft SQL server or Oracle, is needed. For very top performance, where cost is not an issue, Oracle tends to be the best-performing DMBS. The platform the web server is running on is another key factor. If the web server is Windows, then SQL server is likely to be the chosen DBMS; if it is Unix, it is likely to be MySQL or for high performance, Oracle.

Figure 6.8 shows an ASP.NET script that reads data from a particular table in a Microsoft Access database and outputs it to a .NET control, called a DataGrid, to create the web page:

- when this ASP.NET script is called by the server, the Page_Load subroutine (lines 3–14) is executed;

- before a script can issue commands to a DBMS it needs to establish a connection. Line 4 declares the variables that will be used to create the database connection, line 5 makes a connection to the northwind.mdb database file and assigns the connection to the variable dbconn;

- then line 6 opens the connection;

- in line 7, the SQL statement 'SELECT * FROM customers' is executed, which means "give me all the records from the table called 'customers'"; and

- line 8 assigns the returned records to the dbread variable. The ASP.NET DataGrid control in line 18 is a very useful control that becomes a table of results when it is 'bound' to the returned records from the database (lines 9–10) without the need to write any more code.

```
<!DOCTYPE html PUBLIC "-//W3C//DTD XHTML 1.0
   Transitional//EN" "http://www.w3.org/TR/xhtml1/DTD/
   xhtml1-transitional.dtd">
1  <%@ Import Namespace="System.Data.OleDb" %>
2  <script runat="server">
3  sub Page_Load
4  dim dbconn,sql,dbcomm,dbread
5  dbconn=New OleDbConnection("Provider=Microsoft.Jet.
   OLEDB.4.0;data source=" &
          server.mappath("northwind.mdb"))
6  dbconn.Open()
7  dbcomm=New OleDbCommand("SELECT * FROM
   customers",dbconn)
8  dbread=dbcomm.ExecuteReader()
9  northwinddata.DataSource=dbread
10 northwinddata.DataBind
11 dbread.Close
12 dbconn.Close
13 end sub
14 </script>
15 <html xmlns="http://www.w3.org/1999/xhtml">
16 <body>
17 <form runat="server">
18 <asp:DataGrid id="northwinddata" runat="server">
   </asp:DataGrid>
19 </form>
20 </body>
21 </html>
```

*Figure 6.8: An ASP.NET script that reads data from
Northwind database and outputs to a web page*

Figure 6.9 shows how a new record is added to the Northwind database. In this example:

- the contents of the new record are written straight into the SQL statement (line 9), the statement says "create a new record in the 'customers' table and insert these values in the fields 'CustomerID', 'CompanyName' and 'ContactName' ". In practice, the new record would probably come from a form filled out by a user;

- a .NET object called OleDb is used (lines 2–3) to take care of the communication between the script and the database;

- Lines 10–11 create the command to update the database;
- line 12 executes it; and
- line 13 closes the connection to the database.

```
1   <%@ Page Language="vb" %>
2   <%@ import Namespace="System.Data" %>
3   <%@ import Namespace="System.Data.OleDb" %>
4   <script runat="server">
5   Dim dbconn As OleDbConnection
6   Sub Page_Load(Sender As Object, E As EventArgs)
7     dbconn=New OleDbConnection("Provider=Microsoft.Jet.
      OLEDB.4.0;data source="

       & server.mappath("northwind.mdb"))
8     Dim SQLCommand As OleDBCommand

9     Dim InsertCmd As String = "INSERT INTO customers
      (CustomerID, CompanyName,
      ContactName) VALUES ('234', ETC Co', 'G Elliott')"
10    SQLCommand = new OleDbCommand(InsertCmd,dbconn)
11    SQLCommand.Connection.Open()
12    SQLCommand.ExecuteNonQuery()
13    SQLCommand.Connection.Close()
14  End Sub
15  </script>
```

**Figure 6.9: An ASP.NET script that writes a
new record to the Northwind database**

In general, when any script of any language reads or writes to a database it must:

i)   establish a **database connection**;

ii) construct an **SQL statement**;

iii) execute the statement; and finally

iv) close the connection.

> **TIP**
>
> Lecturers do not like to see large extracts of code in assignments, but they do like to see key fragments of code that show what the script or program is doing with an explanation.

6.4: Chapter summary

In general, to support web-based applications, such as an online shop, writing and reading from a database is required. Therefore, web programmers require the skill of designing databases. Dynamic applications often require user information, handled by web forms, to be sent to a web server. Web forms enable user information to be collected with a range of inputs, e.g. checkboxes, text boxes, drop down list, etc. HTTP and scripting languages have standard mechanisms and methods for obtaining the data from a web form and for reading and writing to databases.

6.5: Example questions

1. What does the phrase 'database-driven website' mean and what are the benefits of such a website?

2. How can information be input into a database from a web page?

3. Consider a mail order business selling books that wishes to develop an online store. Briefly, how would an online store such as this work and what issues need to be considered?

6.6: Example answers

1. You need to start by briefly explaining what databases are and their purpose, i.e. storing structured information. You can then explain how databases are used in website design – to generate pages dynamically from information stored in a database. Use an example, such as a members' site, to illustrate how a member would submit their details via a web page form that a server-side script or program would check against a table in a database containing the members' details. The benefits of a database-driven website are that:

   i) information can be stored and retrieved from a database so that each page no longer needs to be manually built in advance; and

   ii) database-driven websites enable sophisticated applications to be built since users can now interact and submit information.

2. This question is essentially asking you to explain how web page forms work. You should be able to illustrate your answer either using HTML as in *Figure 6.4, page 97* explaining how the ACTION attribute works or using a scripting language such as ASP.NET, giving key fragments of code.

3. This is a larger question than the previous two and would probably attract more marks. The question gives you plenty of scope to show what you know about database-driven websites. Start by outlining what information needs to be stored in advance – the book catalogue with prices, categories and details of each book. Then explain how a user would browse through the books for sale and the sequence of events from:

    i)   inputting a search string, e.g. 'books on science' into a web page form;

    ii) the script setting up a link to the books catalogue database;

    iii) retrieving the relevant books; and

    iv) sending back the completed web page. You could also explain a shopping trolley system as described in *Section 6.1, page 94* and *10.1, page 158* would work. A good answer would also explain about validation (*see Figure 6.6, page 100*). The issues that need to be considered are the choice of platform (Windows or Unix), web server (Microsoft IIS or Apache), DBMS (Microsoft Access or SQL server, MySQL or Oracle), depending on the existing hardware configurations of the organisation and the level of traffic that it is expects to receive.

6.7: Further reading and research

Books

Databases, Robert Warrender (2003) ISBN: 1903337089 Lexden Publishing: Colchester.

Websites

Add the number in square brackets to **www.bookref.net/lpwm** for the most up to date web link, for example www.bookref.net/lpwm0110

www.w3schools.com – the w3schools site have many useful tutorials on languages and technologies needed for connecting to a database. [0601]

Chapter 7

WEBSITE DESIGN AND REDESIGN

Chapter overview

The focus of this chapter is on website redesign. However, the techniques used in website redesign also apply to the design process and are therefore explained in this chapter. The main difference between design and redesign is that the experiences and information gained from running an existing site can be useful in the redesign process. Therefore, this chapter also covers some techniques that utilise existing users in the design process. The specific issues of intranet design are also covered.

Learning outcomes

After reading and completing the questions at the end of this chapter (*see page 122*) you should be able to achieve these outcomes:

Outcome 1: Apply the main principles of website design to existing sites.

Outcome 2: Distinguish the differences in website redesign from website design.

Outcome 3: Outline the main principles of intranet design.

How will you be assessed on this?

For coursework you might be given the details of an existing site, or asked to pick an example of a real site for redesigning. You might then be asked to analyse that site and make your recommendations on plan for redesign. In an examination situation you could be given a specific scenario and asked the same question. You would then need to demonstrate your understanding of website design and the issues involved in website redesign.

7.1:   Introduction

The first question that arises when considering redesigning an organisation's website is 'why'? And there could be several good reasons, for example:

- the website may no longer serve its original purpose;

- the design may now look jaded or dated;

- it may not be achieving high ranking in the search engines results;

- the pages many not download fast enough;

- competitors' sites look better;

- the site functionality no longer meets the users' needs;

- the site no longer reaches the target audience;

- the site usability and accessibility do not meet the W3C standards (*see Section 2.2, page 15*).

Section 8.1, page 126 suggests that websites should be reviewed regularly, particularly the technology used. As part of that review, it is also important to consider the reasons listed above. If any of the above statements apply, then some degree of redesign is necessary.

Web design could be the responsibility of just one person or several depending on the size of the organisation and the importance placed on the organisation's site. In organisations of over 200 employees, there is likely to be at least one full-time person responsible for the upkeep of the website. However, in some organisations, responsibility for the website may be contracted out to a specialist website design company. In larger companies there could be a website development team that might include:

Web master	The web master's role may vary in different organisations, but in general it will include the editing and management of the content on the site.
Web designer	The designer is responsible for the look and feel of the site and ensuring it is consistently applied across the site.
Web programmer	If the site is driven via a Content Management System or includes more sophisticated functionality, such as a wish list, then some organisations will need a web programmer.
Graphic designer	If the website is very large, for example the BBC website, then there is a need for the role of someone who designs the entire site's graphics. In smaller organisations this role would be undertaken by the web designer.

Depending on the nature and size of the website, the team might also include a multimedia developer, interface designer and usability engineers.

All websites follow a lifecycle from initial design and launch, a long stable period when the site is maintained with only small changes to content and layout, and finally, a stage of complete site redesign. The long stable period may last several years depending on the nature of the site and the capabilities of an organisation to redesign it. Clearly, the redesign of a website must be undertaken at the same time as maintaining the existing site.

In the rest of this chapter it is the main techniques and approaches of website design and redesign that are covered.

7.2: Website design – basic techniques

This section covers some of the basic techniques used for website design, but in the context of redesigning a site. The first step in website design is understanding the needs of the visitor to a site by undertaking a **user needs analysis**, to which several techniques can be applied. In the first instance, it is important for designers to have a clear idea of all the types of people who use their sites and to categorise them into particular groups. For new websites this task is difficult, but for existing sites, information about visitors to the site can be gained by asking them to complete a short online questionnaires including, for example, age, gender and reason for visiting site. In addition, websites should be set up to capture usage data via tools such as Google Analytics (**www.google.co.uk/analytics/**) (*see also Chapter 9, pages 139–156* for information on gathering site usage statistics). From this information the designer should be able to categorise people who visit the site, their reasons for visiting and the most popular pages accessed.

Another useful technique is to produce **user scenarios** that try to imagine how each type of visitor might interact with the site. Scenarios are simply descriptions of the typical way each visitor type might interact with the site, which pages they might visit, in what order and what they would want to obtain from the site. *Figure 7.1* shows a typical scenario of someone visiting an online rare books shop.

- Bill usually buys his books on Amazon, but has been unable to find a particular book he has been hunting for.

- Bill notices a link to the rare bookshop after carrying out an Internet-wide search using a popular search engine and follows the link.

- When he arrives at the rare book site, Bill looks at the home page to see if there is a search function available on the site, but it is not immediately obvious so he clicks on the link for 'catalogue'.

- In the catalogue section the books are listed via categorised links and Bill tries a few of these, but without success. Then he notices the search engine in the top left-hand corner of the book categories page and enters the title of the book, again without success.

- Getting frustrated, Bill clicks on the advanced search link and enters the ISBN number of the book.

- The search engine recognises the ISBN, but it is not in stock and Bill gives up.

Figure 7.1: A scenario of someone using a rare books online shop

Compiling this information with a series of scenarios enables the designer to determine how the site should be organised and structured to most easily support user needs. For example, the scenario in *Figure 7.1* shows that the search function needs to be clearer and perhaps include the ISBN of the books in the basic search function.

There are two useful tools that are helpful in the process of organising and structuring the site, **structure diagrams** or **charts** and **flowcharts**. *Figure 7.2* shows a typical structure diagram of part of a rare books shop site where each box represents a page or section of the site. Clearly, when considering an existing site, the structure already exists, so it is a case of reviewing it with the use of a structure diagram.

Structure diagrams can quickly become over complicated so usually they are broken down into separate pages for sections and subsections, but with a general structure diagram covering the overall site with references to each section diagram. So, for example, in *Figure 7.2* there would need to be a link from the 'Sciences' box to a separate structure diagram just for 'Sciences'.

Examining structure diagrams enables designers to work out whether there should be any changes to the structure of the site considering the previous analysis of usage patterns and scenarios.

Flowcharts are another useful tool when designing sites as they can illustrate a sequence of activities such as 'ordering of a product' from a site. *Figure 7.3* shows the symbols used in flowcharts and *Figure 7.4* shows a typical example.

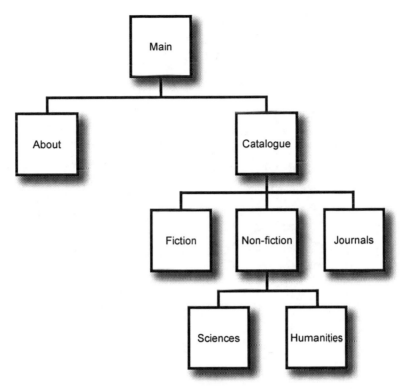

Figure 7.2: Example structure diagram for a online rare books shop

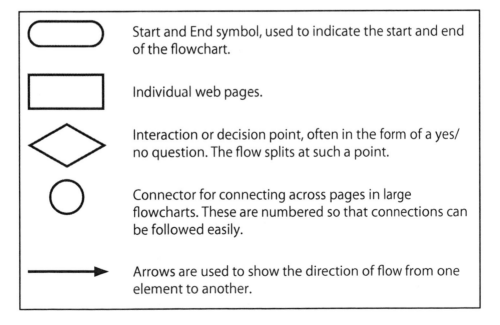

Figure 7.3: Symbols used in flowcharts

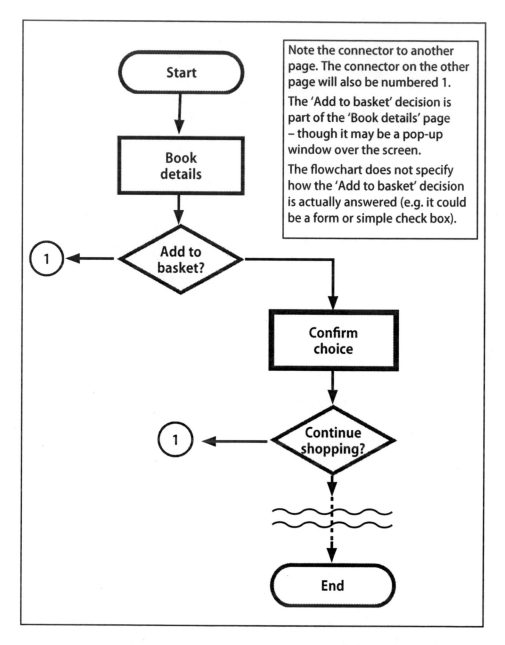

Start

Book details

Note the connector to another page. The connector on the other page will also be numbered 1.

The 'Add to basket' decision is part of the 'Book details' page – though it may be a pop-up window over the screen.

The flowchart does not specify how the 'Add to basket' decision is actually answered (e.g. it could be a form or simple check box).

Add to basket?

1

Confirm choice

Continue shopping?

1

End

Figure 7.4: A flowchart of the process of buying a book

Once the designers are happy with the structure or restructure of the site they can turn to the structure and layout of each page. The standard technique used for helping in the design of page layouts are **storyboards** or **wireframes** that are simply sketches of a how the page might appear as shown in the example in *Figure 7.5*.

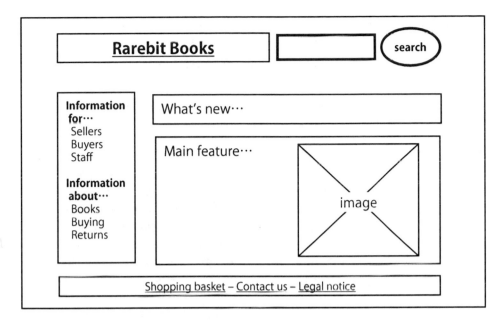

Figure 7.5: Storyboard of the homepage for a rare books site

Clearly, for an existing site the storyboards may be used to look at varying degrees of redesign, from just moving a few page elements around to a complete site redesign. Often, professional designers will use an image-editing tool, such as Adobe Photoshop, to create the storyboards. Once the layout and look and feel have been agreed, a storyboard created in an image editor can be quickly converted into a web page.

7.3: Other techniques

Redesigning an existing site means that the experiences gained from running it can inform the redesign process. A review of the existing site can be conducted by a selected panel of people including a technical person, someone from marketing, and perhaps, someone more senior in the organisation. This panel can systematically review each page or section of the existing site and determine what is wrong or right about it. One approach is for the panel to compile a list of important factors, or **heuristics**, it wished to use as checklist. The panel can then assess the **usability** of the site, i.e. how easy is the site to use against each heuristic and then recommend ways in which the new site could improve on the old one. Typical heuristics might include:

- **Consistency** – is the design, layout and navigation consistent?

- **Visible status information** – does the site clearly help the visitor know where in the site they are and what they need to do next?

- **Minimalist design** – does the site or page contain irrelevant or redundant information?

- **Error prevention** – do error-prone conditions require confirmation before visitors are committed to an action?

- **Match between system and the real world** – does the site use words, phrases and concepts familiar to the user?

- **User control and freedom** – does the site help visitors who make mistakes to get back on track easily?

(*See Chapter 11, pages 169–180* for more detail regarding usability.)

Another important and useful technique that can be employed is to include visitors' feedback and comments in the redesign process. Feedback can be obtained from visitors in several ways, for example you can add online forms to the website to capture user comments. Also by implementing Google Analytics or analysing the server logs with tools, such as Matrix Stats, or you can see which pages are most important to visitors and therefore restructure the site emphasising these pages. You can also involve visitors in a more formal way by inviting them to participate in the redesign process. You can make early versions of the new website available to selected visitors and ask them to send in their feedback via e-mail or online forms. Using real users in the redesign process is called **participative design** and it makes it possible to significantly improve the usability of the new site. Ideally, if you can arrange for real users to be available in person during key stages in the design process, it is possible to be more structured in obtaining their opinions. It is possible to observe users using the prototypes of the new site and ask them questions about their experiences.

Personalisation and customisation

There has been a growing interest in recent years in **personalised** and **customised** websites. Personalised web pages are those where the website displays tailored content based on knowledge gathered on previous visits either automatically (i.e. which pages and links did they last visit or use) or explicitly by asking visitors for their preferences. Customised websites are those where the user can make choices about what and how they view a site, which might include: the content, links and layout and appearance. Both personalisation and customisation require significant server-side programming for them to be implemented. However, there are content management applications available, such as Drupal (*see Section 8.3, page 128* for more details), that have some of the required functionality already built in.

A good example of personalisation can be found on the **amazon.co.uk** site. It has a personalised welcome back message and features that remind you of the items that you looked at during your last visit and makes suggestions based on similarly categorised items (*see Figure 7.6.*)

Acknowledgement of the name of the user

Record of previous viewed items

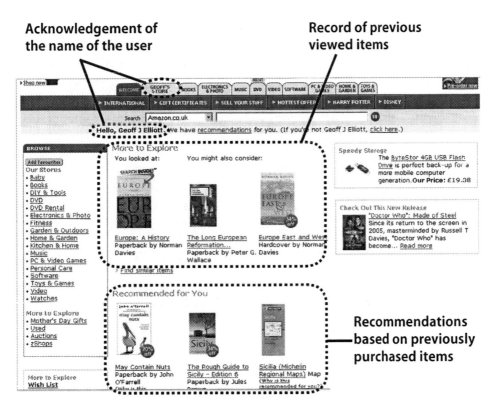

Recommendations based on previously purchased items

Figure 7.6: Example of personalisation

There are three ways to personalise a website:

Rule based	Pre-defined rules built into the website code that respond to particular visitor-driven events, e.g. 'if the user visits this sequence of particular pages then display this link to news item'. Building the rules into the code makes this approach inflexible and difficult to maintain.
Collaborative filtering	This works on the basis of what other people have clicked on, selected or bought. The examples in *Figures 7.7a* and *b* are based on collaborative filtering. This approach relies on a large enough group of visitors in order to make relevant and valid suggestions to the visitor.
Inference	This works by developing a profile of visitors, based on what they click on, the choices they make, the pages they visit and the order in which they are visited. Based on this information, the web server can 'infer' what each visitor is likely to be interested in and modify the content accordingly. Developing an inferencing application requires significant programming and understanding of how inferencing works.

There are commercial and open source applications and tools that can be installed on the server that can provide personalisation functionality, some of which are listed in the references. However, these tools still need to be tailored and programmed for specific uses.

Google and Yahoo (**www.yahoo.com**) are good examples of sites where visitors can arrange the layout of their main page and add extra elements such as the latest news. Some sites also offer visitors the opportunity to change the size and colour of the typeface to display and the background colour in order to increase the accessibility of their sites. For example, **www.visionaustralia. org.au** has two links at the top of their home page for visitors to change the text size and the level of contrast (*see Figure 7.7a and b*). This feature can be implemented relatively easily using CSS and cookies.

Figure 7.7a: The visionaustralia.org.au website with standard font size and contrast

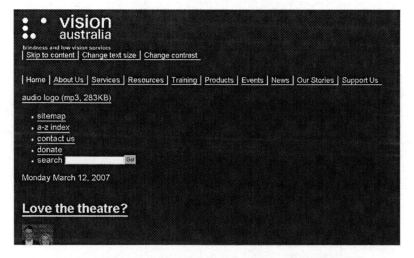

Figure 7.7b: The visionaustralia.org.au website with

large font and high contrast

7.4: Intranet design

Intranets can mean different things to different people, but in general they are 'private versions of the Internet' designed for individual organisations. Intranets use the Internet protocol suite to help integrate an organisation's:

- networks;
- file servers;
- communication systems (e.g. e-mail);
- work processes (e.g. requesting leave); and
- documentation or knowledge.

Ideally, all the functions of an intranet can be accessed via a single 'home' web page. The design of an intranet is a little different from that of an external focussed website in that:

i)   they are generally more complex and involve integrating more than one application or function; and

ii)   the various people who will use and update it are on-hand and should contribute to its development.

Most organisations over a certain size will have intranets almost by default since they will already have a network, file servers, e-mail, and some electronic documentation. The problem with this approach is that it is unplanned and unstructured and it is unclear what the purpose of such an intranet is. Therefore the first step in designing an intranet is to develop an intranet strategy that identifies the purposes it should serve and will include some or all of the following:

- improve productivity by helping employees to quickly find and view information and applications relevant to their job whenever they need it;
- provide knowledge and information to employees when they need it. It is more efficient for employees to go to the source, rather than produce multiple copies sent to everyone;
- provide search facilities to all material on the intranet;
- support collaborative working and communication up and down and across an organisation;
- enable large organisational documents, e.g. procedures, to be easily maintained and searched; and
- improve business processes.

The next step is to establish a development team that includes the technical people, representatives of the various functional areas of the organisation and also representatives from each level of management. The first job of the development team is to agree the **requirement specification** for the intranet. Following this, the technical people can identify the technical solution necessary to implement the requirements and, at the same time, the designers can start storyboarding the look of the intranet pages.

The rules and guidelines governing layout of an intranet home page are very similar as for a conventional website. The key differences are likely to be the extra details and additional links required on the intranet home page for all the extra functionality. Intranet pages are used on a daily basis by people in the organisation so there is no need to include flashy graphics; the important principle is that it is highly useable. The key principles for the design of intranet pages are:

- consistency of layout, navigation, use of typefaces throughout site and ensuring each area or department is forced to adhere to the standards;

- Information should only appear on an Intranet site once and then hyperlinked to from anywhere else that refers to the same information;

- it is better to structure the site in line with the needs of the staff and their work processes rather than by the organisational structure.

Ideally, the management of the intranet should be by a core team with one person (such as the web master) with overall control. However, the day-to-day operation and development of the intranet should be devolved to people across the organisation. This means the only effective way to implement an intranet is to use a Content Management System (CMS) that incorporates a user-management system as detailed in *Section 8.3, page 128*. The user-management system means people can 'log onto' the intranet and update content dynamically without the need for any technical skills. How intranets are implemented is covered in *Section 4.4, page 71*.

7.5: Design issues

There are a number of other factors that need to be considered when designing or redesigning websites. As noted in *Section 8.4, page 130*, it is important to undertake an analysis of browser versions, colour depth and screen resolutions used by visitors to your site because any redesigning of your site should take these differences into account. For instance, if 40% of your visitors still use a screen resolution of 800 x 600 pixels per inch (ppi) you should ensure that your new designs display properly at this resolution. If, on the other hand, less than 10% use a screen resolution of 800 x 600 ppi you might choose to optimise your designs for a higher resolution.

If you are redesigning a site that uses a CMS, you must be aware of any limitations that it may have on your designs. Typically, for a CMS to work, all pages have a fixed layout and screen areas where the designer may have no choice over layout.

Design of search function

Most people quickly resort to using the search feature if they cannot quickly find what they want by navigating around a site. Therefore, the design of a site's search function is critical to ensuring that visitors can use the site effectively. Here are some key guidelines In designing a search function:

- it should appear on every page in the same location (top right is very common);

- the text entry box should be at least 20 or 30 characters to allow visitors to type their search term; and

- it should be possible to refine searches by limiting them to particular sections of the site.

The way in which the results are displayed is also critical:

- ensure the layout of the results is clear and in order of relevance;

- each entry on the results page should include the page title and a summary;

- illustrate the relationship between the search terms and the page by listing and highlighting the fragments of the page that include the search term in the page summary;

- include the number of pages found with the search term;

- include another 'search again' feature because people invariably will wish to do this; and

- include a link to the site map.

If the search does not find any matches, it is important to explain why this may have occurred and offer other suggestions such as re-enter the search term, advice on the construction of the search term or even contacting the site owner.

If you wish to include an advanced search function, provide a link to a help page that explains all its features. Offer visitors user-friendly ways of carrying out 'boolean' searches, for example by adding radio button options that allow matches on 'any word', 'all words' and 'precise phrase'.

7.6: Chapter summary

All websites have a lifecycle and need to be partially or fully redesigned at some point. Web design or redesign is undertaken by a team of people that can include amongst others a designer, programmer and graphic designer. Website redesign utilises many of the same techniques used in initial site design, e.g. storyboarding, structure diagrams, flowcharts. The difference is the access to the existing customer or visitor base who can participate by commenting on the new designs and site structure. More advanced techniques can be employed including conducting usability studies and adding personalisation and customisation features to the site. The design of intranets has some specific design issues because of the complexity of the requirements and a systematic approach with contributions from people across an organisation is required.

7.7: Example questions

1. What are the differences between designing a website from the beginning and redesigning an existing site?

2. You have been brought in as a consultant to a company selling rare books over the web. The company has had its website for several years, but in the last 12 months sales have begun to fall away. The company has asked you for advise. How can you redesign the site to improve the company's sales?

7.8: Example answers

1. The purpose of this question is to ascertain if you understand the differences between design and redesign. The basic techniques for the redesign of a site are the same as those for designing, e.g. storyboards, structure diagrams and flowcharts. However, since there is an existing site, the key differences are:

    *   access to performance data on the existing site including statistics on:

        *   the number of visits to each page on the site, indicating their importance in the eyes of visitors,

        *   the types browsers, computers, screen resolutions and colour depths used; and

        *   where the visitors are being referred from;

    *   access to a number of current site visitors who could help in the redesign process by providing feedback on draft designs via e-mail or web forms.

    A small number of existing site users could be invited to be actively involved in the redesign process, i.e. participative design.

2. The first step in the design process is to review the existing site by bringing together a number of individuals from the organisation to form a review panel. You might instruct the panel to compile a list of heuristics to review the site. At the same time, the data from the web server log files needs to be analysed to determine which pages are least and most used as well as helping to develop a profile of typical visitors. The next step might be to start thinking about how the new site should be structured by using

structure diagrams alongside the analysis of the server logs. If the site is an online shop or service (e.g. uploading a document for processing), you might suggest using a flowchart to redesign the stages required to buy something or use the service. Having completed these exercises you should be in a position to redesign the page layouts using storyboards and the results of the panel review of the existing site.

If the existing site does not use a Content Management System, you might want to recommend that the rare books company considers whether it should build the new site using such a system and suggest one or two for them to consider.

7.9: Further reading and research

Books

Cunliffe, D and Elliott, G. (2005) *Multimedia Computing*, Lexden Publishing: Colchester.

Websites

Add the number in square brackets to **www.bookref.net/lpwm** for the most up to date web link, for example www.bookref.net/lpwm0110

www.criteo.com – is a company that provides an inference application. [0701]

http://taste.sourceforge.net – is an open source collaborative filtering application. [0702]

www.netmag.co.uk/zine/design-culture/how-to-redesign-a-website/ – magazine article on website redesign. [0703]

www.boagworld.com/archives/2006/05/creating_a_great_search_facility.html – an article on designing a search facility. [0704]

www.bestpricecomputers.co.uk/glossary/intranet-strategies.htm – an article on compiling an intranet strategy. [0705]

www.merges.net/theory/20010402.html – an article on personalisation. [0706]

http://en.wikipedia.org/wiki/intranet/ – the Wikipedia entry on intranets. [0707]

Chapter 8

WEBSITE MAINTENANCE

Chapter overview

The content of most websites will need to be updated on a regular basis. Redesigns of the site are required occasionally to freshen up the appearance and to ensure the site meets the latest web standards. In this chapter, we cover the essential principles of website maintenance that anyone who manages a website should adopt.

Learning outcomes

You should already be familiar with building web pages for assignment purposes as part of your course. Once a site has been built, maintaining it is crucial. However, unless you already manage a site, it will be difficult to gain much practical experience of maintaining one. Therefore, the outcomes for this chapter explain the principles and processes of website maintenance. After studying this chapter and answering the example questions at the end (*see page 135*) you should be able to achieve these outcomes:

Outcome 1: Explain the issues related to website maintenance.

Outcome 2: Outline the website maintenance process.

How will you be assessed on this?

In an examination question you would be asked to explain what website maintenance is and the process for undertaking it. You might be given a particular case study or scenario for a site needing maintenance and be asked to come up with an appropriate strategy.

8.1: Introduction

A large part of website management is the process of website maintenance, which includes:

- checking that the content and links are correct and working;

- reviewing and managing the growth of the content of the site;

- reviewing the look and feel of the site and modifying as required;

- ensuring the web server hardware is fit for its purpose and upgrading, if necessary;

- ensuring that the web server system software is up to date and all appropriate patches, upgrades and service packs are installed;

- ensuring that the website meets acceptable performance levels in terms of download speed, usability, cross-browser compatibility;

- ensuring that the technologies used to the build website remain standards-compliant and continuously migrate to current accepted standards; and

- ensuring that the site meets all legal requirements.

Websites that are not maintained will begin to look tired, and out-of-date content will not impress visitors. Worse still, the site may stop displaying or functioning properly in newer versions of browsers.

These activities need to be undertaken systematically and periodically. Some are trivial and can be automated or semi-automated and some require significant effort. In the rest of this chapter, we examine what these activities mean and how they are carried out.

In any organisation, there should be one person with overall responsibility for the IT systems including the website(s) – the Systems Manager. Then, depending on the size of the organisation, there needs to be someone responsible for all the hardware, someone for the operating system and other software, maybe someone for specialised servers such as those hosting databases and then someone with overall responsibility for the content and running of the website – the **Web Master**. In smaller organisations, the web master's role might be part of another role. In some organisations the web master's role is more technical; in others it is more to do with managing the content. Often, the technical role and the content management role are separated.

8.2: Content management

Managing the content of a small website is usually not a problem, but as the size of a site grows, the task quickly becomes overwhelming and a systematic approach is required. The key to managing the content of larger websites is to store and deliver the content from a database using server-side programming to read and write to the database. Applications specifically designed for this purpose are called **Content Management Systems (CMS)** and are described in detail in *Section 8.3, page 128. Chapter 6, pages 93–107* also explains how databases and server-side programming are used to deliver web content to a browser. Regardless of whether a site is driven by a CMS or is a static set of web pages, the principles of content management remain important. The content of a site must be checked for:

a) erroneous content;

b) broken links, both internal and external;

c) consistency of the look and feel;

d) consistent navigation throughout site;

e) satisfactory function of site search engine if present;

f) up-to-date site map;

g) up-to-date policy documents for copyright, terms of use, privacy statement, accessibility, etc.;

h) any date references, e.g. pages that refer to an event that has already passed;

i) updating keywords and page meta data;

j) correct e-mail addresses;

k) update automated messages; and

l) working web forms.

Some of these tasks can be automated, for instance there are applications that can be installed that will periodically check for broken links and there are sites that will check a site for broken links for free, e.g. **www.dead-links.com**. With a CMS, a site map can be produced dynamically from the database and programs can be written to search the database for content that refers to dates. However, some tasks, for example a), c), d), g), i), j) and l) above, can only be carried by humans. To undertake these, it is a good idea to have a **content maintenance schedule** for the routine tasks that are to be completed periodically by set dates. The schedule could mean work being carried out on each section of the site simultaneously. A good CMS can make this task easier by enabling more than one person to update the site simultaneously, which means being able to delegate responsibilities for the tasks or sections of the site to other individuals under the control of one over-arching editor (the web master).

In the same way that the checking of existing content must be systematic, so must the addition of new content. Ideally, a process should be in place so that anyone who wants to add content or restructure content sends the details of the update to the person responsible for that section of the site, who decides whether to include the new content and edits it for conformance to a house style. This process may involve several people approving the new content, for example the head of department or someone with legal responsibilities.

8.3: Content Management Systems

Maintenance of content is often done by a few designated people, e.g. the web master or a web design company (that probably charge a fee every time a change is made). Anyone wishing to make changes may have to wait their turn until the designated people can make them. If changes are still carried out using a web page editor, these could be time consuming and create potential bottlenecks, leading to out of date websites. If there were a change of personnel or design company, then there is a high probability that page layouts become inconsistent and the quality of presentation difficult to maintain. Solutions, known as **Content Management Systems (CMS)**, have evolved to let organisations maintain their websites more efficiently without the need of a web design company or web design expertise.

A CMS is an application that runs on a web server and allows users to generate and maintain websites by storing the page content, links and structure in a database, as shown in *Figure 8.1*. In order to set-up the website initially, designated web developers create the page layout templates for the whole site and install and set-up any functionality that is required, such as the search engine, and apply the access rights (including the editing and reviewing), using the CMS tools. Content authors can then log into the CMS through a web page interface, created by the designers and start to adding content or making changes, This might include adding text and images, sound, video files, links to other sites and the navigational structure.

Unlike web page design tools, such as Adobe Dreamweaver, where developers have complete control over each page they design, in a CMS, content authors create pages by filling out web forms to define the content, links, etc. This means that the content authors do not need to be web page design experts or know anything about HTML. Usually, there is at least one user who is designated as a CMS administrator whose job it is to create and maintain all the accounts for the developers and content authors to log in.

Some large-scale CMSs also manage the workflow process of approving and maintaining pages. This means, for example, that the CMS automatically sends a notification e-mail to the person who needs to approval a newly-made change. Any changed or new pages remain 'pending' until approved and then are released for general viewing. To approve changes, the approver logs in, examines the pending pages and then amends their status to 'approved'.

So far, we have been considering the **content authoring system**, the other element of a CMS is the **content delivery system**, which manages the display of the website to visitors and users. Depending on the nature of the site, the content delivery system may require visitors to log on before they can see certain parts of the site. For example, in the case of an organisational intranet, the content delivery system can be set to determine which pages the users can see, for instance sales staff could access the human resource department's policies, but not their personnel records.

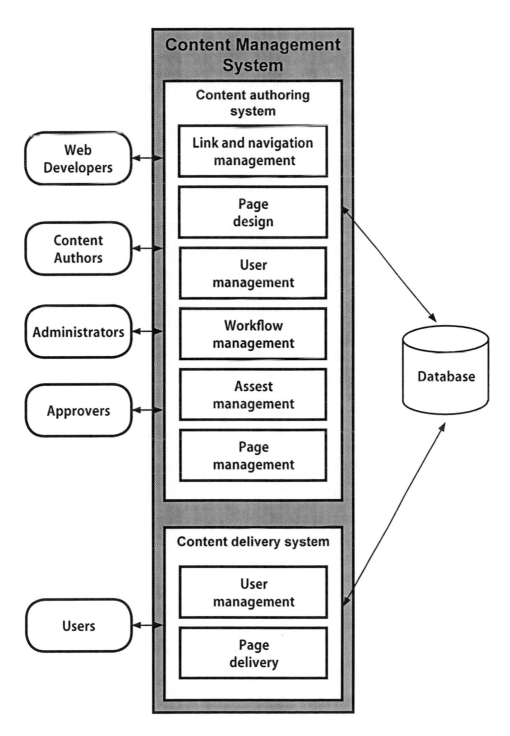

Figure 8.1: Structure of a Content Management System

In summary, the benefits of using a CMS are:

- the control over the content can be placed with those responsible for creating it rather than web developers, e.g. the marketing development rather than the IT department;

- workflow is often included in the application ensuring quality rules are adhered to;

- it provides a consistent page design across the site;

- a search engine is often included in the application and can be added to the site;

- the layout and design of the whole site can be changed instantly, if a new design layout has been completed either internally or externally.

There are many CMSs available to build websites, many are commercial, but many are also open source, i.e. free to install and use. Some of the most popular open source CMSs, e.g. Drupal, Xoops and Xaraya, are used by many large, well-known organisations around the world. The site – **www.opensourcecms.com** contains details of the majority of the open source CMS in use.

8.4: Web standards and technology review

The web technologies used for creating web pages, the browsers designed for displaying pages and any associated standards evolve and change rapidly. It is therefore important to review the current state of technology and evaluate your website to ensure it meets the latest standards and technology requirements. It is important to do this because your web pages may no longer display correctly. These reviews probably only need to be undertaken once or twice a year or when a significant change is to be made to your website.

Chapter 2, pages 13–34 explains some of the new standards – XHTML, CSS and XML, but there are many others that may have an impact on your website. The W3C site has details of all the accepted and developing standards and it has mailing lists that you can join and receive details of any new developments, *see Further reading and research, page 136* for further details. You should periodically resubmit your website to any validation services that you declare your site to be compliant with.

You might also want to check how your website appears in various makes and versions of browser, especially those most popular with your users. Browser usage varies considerably over time, especially when a new version of a browser is released. For example, Internet Explorer 7 was released in October 2006 so although its usage started low (4% of all browsers in 2006) it will grow rapidly. Mozilla Firefox has been steadily increasing in popularity since its launch in 2005. The overall breakdown of browser usage in 2006 was approximately:

80-85%	Internet Explorer (roughly 4% IE7, 4% IE5 and 72% IE6)
10-15%	Mozilla Firefox
1-2%	Apple Safari
<1%	Opera
<1%	Netscape (all versions)

Browser usage will also vary between different websites, for instance users of a site dedicated to Unix development issues will generally prefer Firefox or Opera over Internet Explorer. It is therefore important that you have these statistics available for your website so that you can ensure your site displays properly in the browsers that your visitors use. *Chapter 9, pages 139–155*, outlines the need to capture website usage statistics for marketing purposes, but it is also possible to capture the types and versions of browsers, operating systems, screen resolutions and colour depths used by people accessing your site. *Figure 8.2* shows a typical table of screen resolution statistics gathered using the Google Analytics website monitoring tool. This data helps ensure that a site meets the needs of its users, for example *Figure 8.2* indicates that 10% of visitors are still using a resolution of 800 x 600 ppi, so page designs must still take this into account.

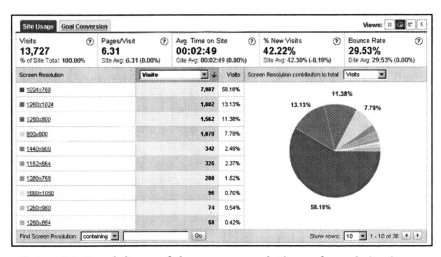

Figure 8.2: Breakdown of the screen resolutions of a websites' users monitored by Google Analytics

Ideally, once a year it is worth testing the download speed of a sample of your pages, perhaps those indicated as the most popular in the site statistics. The download speed of pages will vary from one moment to the next in response to network variations, so the test should be carried out several times, perhaps over an hour period, and an average taken. The browser cache needs to be cleared after every visit and then closed down and reopened. If the average download time is less than one or two seconds, then nothing needs to be done. It is also worth repeating this exercise with the most popular browsers used to access your site.

8.5: Hardware and system software maintenance

The effect of the hardware and system software on the performance of a website is critical. For many sites, this is the responsibility of the hosting company. However, when you contract to have your website hosted, you should ensure that the service you select promises to undertake a regular maintenance routine and review of hardware and system software. It is also useful, periodically, to ask your hosting company to confirm what maintenance activities have been taking place. Websites rely not just on the web server computer, but also the server computers hosting the databases, the Domain Name System and various other computers. Therefore, every computer involved in delivering the website to the end-user must be maintained.

The first key activity is keeping all server and system software up to date. As bugs and security weaknesses in the software are discovered, the originating organisation produces **patches** – small modifications to their software to fix the problems. These can be downloaded from the appropriate website, but on Windows-based computers there is an application 'Windows Update' that will automatically check for any necessary upgrades over the Internet. There are similar applications for Unix-based computers (e.g. Linux) for example Sun Microsystems 'Update Connection'.

The performance of servers needs to be monitored regularly and for heavily-used servers this should be done daily. On Windows-based servers this is done with the **Windows Task Manager** (*see Figure 8.3*) There are more sophisticated applications available for extra detailed monitoring. A useful technique is to monitor each server for a period of time under normal operating conditions and record the profile of performance, e.g. a specific organisation may decide 'maximum CPU usage 78%, average CPU usage 34%'. This is called the **Performance Baseline**, so when a server starts performing outside the baseline, e.g. maximum CPU usage 95%, then some action needs to be taken. Some monitoring utilities allow you to automate this and set **alerts** when the server goes below or above threshold values. Alerts can be sent as e-mails to designated people.

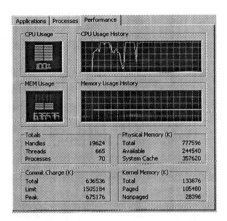

Figure 8.3: Performance monitor of Windows-based server

If you find that the overall system performance is not acceptable, you can identify which process is causing the performance issue using Windows Task Manager (or the Unix equivalent), which enables you to monitor the CPU time and memory usage of each application and system process and hence the problem process can be investigated and remedial action taken. This might include:

- checking that all appropriate software upgrades and patches have been installed;

- upgrading hardware, in particular memory, disk space and/or the network cards; and

- emptying log files. Many applications maintain log file of transactions and activities and over time, they can become very large.

Upgrading hardware and software can be time consuming and costly, and ad hoc upgrades should be avoided. System managers should plan for upgrades in their schedule of maintenance activities and the budgets for the following year. In order to do this, system managers need to estimate the projected levels of usage of servers and then evaluate whether the servers will be sufficient to cope, based on the current performance characteristics of the server.

Disaster recovery planning

A key part of maintaining the server is **disaster recovery planning**, which is the process of planning for unexpected events such as a power or system failure or fire. The disaster recovery plan is a document distributed to all personnel who would be involved with the chain of command in the event of a disaster. The plan should provide clear details of the steps to be taken to recover systems and should include:

- the contact information of all involved personnel and organisations;

- the people designated to initiate the plan;

- the location of backup media; and

- the detailed procedures for restoring computing services.

The procedures for backing up each critical server need to be documented and agreed. 'Backing up' means copying all or key parts of the content of a computer to some form of digital media such as magnetic tape. The frequency of backup will depend on the level of activity on a server and the importance of the content it holds. Any backup media should be stored at a separate, off-site location to minimise the disaster, for example if the servers were destroyed by fire you would still have the data files ready to install on a new server.

Server security

The security of servers is an important element of the maintenance cycle. The patches and fixes that are periodically applied to servers often relate to security weaknesses in the software. It is vital that good anti-virus and spyware software is installed and real-time security monitoring and scheduled system scans are switched on. All passwords associated with the server should be changed regularly and **strong passwords** should be used. Strong passwords are:

- long – over 15 characters; and

- complex – avoiding dictionary words, but include numbers and symbols, lower and upper case characters.

- A pass phrase – in which some characters are replaced with numbers and symbols. For example using the phrase 'the chair of my auntie' to make:

'tH3 cha1r 0f m$ @untie'

Other security measures that should be in place include:

- disabling unnecessary services;

- disabling or deleting unnecessary accounts;

- protecting files and directories;

- making sure the guest account is disabled;

- protecting the registration from anonymous access;

- setting an account lockout policy;

- revoking the debug program's user right;

- removing all unnecessary file shares; and

- enabling security event auditing.

Microsoft has a free tool available to analyse the security status of Windows-based computers called the **Baseline Security Analyzer** that can be used to review the security status of your computers and servers, details are listed in *Further reading and resources, page 136.*

8.6: Chapter summary

Website maintenance means maintenance of the content and of the hardware and system software; it needs to be systematic and planned. Each aspect of the website must be scheduled for review, e.g. any forms on the website checked every three months. For larger websites, a Content Management System is essential to keep content up to date and the responsibilities for each area of the site should be delegated. Ensuring that the website complies with the latest standards is important to guarantee the site displays correctly in new releases of browsers. It is important to continually monitor developments in technology and then plan for upgrading the site in the future. The security of servers is critical and system managers must ensure that potential malicious attacks are made as difficult as possible. There should be a disaster recovery plan in place, particularly for websites running important applications, such as online shops, to ensure that there is minimal disruption to service following any disaster.

8.7: Example questions

1. You work as the webmaster for a greeting cards business that has an online shop. The company was very quick off the mark with selling online and was very successful, but now sales are beginning to drop off even though it is near the top of search engines' search results. What could the reasons for this be and what measures do you think you should take to try to reverse this trend?

2. What are Content Management Systems, how do they operate and what benefits to the greeting cards business (*see question 1 above*) would there be in migrating their site to one?

3. You have been asked to advise your institution on its website. The institution is having trouble keeping the website up to date with the continuous stream of changes required. How could you improve the situation?

8.8: Example answers

1. This question is designed to tease out all you know about website maintenance (but not about any product pricing or quality issues). Since the site is probably quite old, the technology it is based on will also be old and likewise its design, both of which are likely to put off anyone visiting the site. Therefore, the first step is to review what technology upgrade options there are, e.g. migrating the site to XHTML and CSS and consider a redesign of the site as considered in *Chapter 2, page 13* and *Chapter 7, see page 109 – 137*. The next step is to audit the content of the site and check that it is correct and relevant and then arrange for someone to order a greetings card from the site, which will check that everything functions correctly. The old site is unlikely to be standards-compliant, which may be causing problems with some versions of browser. Therefore, an essential activity is to ensure that the site is made compliant. Standards-compliance could be built in from the beginning if the site is to be redesigned.

Another reason for the drop off in business may be the download speed of site's web pages, which might be due to the servers on which the site is hosted. Therefore, it is important to check what arrangements the hosting company has for maintaining and securing its servers. It may be necessary to transfer the site to a better hosting company that can guarantee better service and maintenance arrangements.

2. For the first part of this question start by explaining how website content can be stored in a database. Then reproduce the diagram in *Figure 8.1, page 129* and explain the mechanics of a CMS. The key benefits to the greeting cards company gained by using a CMS are that:

- the site can be updated more easily without relying on a design company to make changes;

- updating areas of the site can be delegated to the appropriate people;

- a search facility can be added; and

- it is easier to keep standards-compliant.

3. This is another question about Content Management Systems. Start by pointing out the general benefits of using a CMS:

- allowing multiple authors with no knowledge of web development to update or create content;

- controlling the process by which content is added or amended.

You will need to explain how a CMS works, perhaps reproducing *Figure 8.1, page 129*. A good answer should give some examples of how a CMS would affect an individual department such as the one you study or work in. Individual lecturers would be able to maintain their own pages, although perhaps the release of content would be controlled by other people in the department, for example a senior administrator or someone from the marketing department. The people responsible for course information for new students would be able to maintain their own pages and update them quickly as new courses are introduced.

8.9: Further reading and research

Websites
Add the number in square brackets to **www.bookref.net/lpwm** for the most up to date web link, for example www.bookref.net/lpwm0110

www.dead-links.com – is a free service for checking for broken links on websites. [0801]

www.w3.org/Mail/ – the page for joining various W3C mailing lists. [0802]

www.google.com/analytics/ – a free tool for website monitoring. [0803]

www.microsoft.com/technet/prodtechnol/windows2000serv/reskit/core/

fneb_mon_ifqs.mspx?mfr=true – guidance on performance monitoring of Windows-based servers. [0804]

www.microsoft.com/technet/security/tools/mbsahome.mspx – is the download for the Microsoft Baseline Security Analyser tool for helping determining the security state of a computer system. [0805]

www.opensourcecms.com – is a site dedicated to all open source Content Management Systems. [0806]

http://drupal.org – a popular open source Content Management System [0807].

Chapter 9

WEBSITE MARKETING

Chapter overview

Whatever your website's purpose, if it is directly available over the web, you will want people to view it. Considering the current size of the World Wide Web, it is not an easy task to make a new website known. The process of getting a website known and indexed or listed by the various search engines and directories is called **website marketing** and requires continuous and systematic effort over many months and years. Website marketing starts with:

i)   developing a strategy plan;

ii) implementing the plan with a number of activities including web page design, search engine and directory submissions, e-mail marketing; and

iii) gathering information about who visits a site and what they view, and then making any necessary adjustments to the plan.

For businesses, website marketing should be part of the whole marketing strategy.

Learning outcomes

After studying this chapter and answering the example questions at the end of the chapter (*see page 154*), you should aim to achieve these outcomes:

Outcome 1: Develop a website marketing strategy.

Outcome 2: Implement a website marketing strategy.

Outcome 3: Monitor a website marketing strategy.

How will you be assessed on this?

In coursework you might be asked to create a website, such as a e-zine, and as a part of that work you might be asked to produce a short website marketing strategy. Alternatively, you might receive an assignment that is specifically about developing a website marketing strategy based on a brief, for example promoting a new course at your college. You might be asked to do a similar thing in an exam.

9.1:   Website marketing strategy

The website marketing strategy should only be part of the organisation's normal marketing strategy, but unless your website is well known and receiving sufficient traffic it will not become an effective part of the overall strategy. Therefore, it is important to have a separate website marketing strategy as well. However, before you can start writing such a strategy, you must already have agreed the organisation's marketing strategy with aims and objectives upon which to base the website marketing strategy. For example, the marketing strategy might include the following objectives:

"To increase sales by 10% per year."

"To be known as one of the top four companies in the sector within three years."

This might translate into the website marketing strategy objectives as:

"To increase traffic to the site to 50 visits per day."

"To be listed in the top two pages of Google, Yahoo and MSN search results using these specific search words and phrases..."

Once you have the objectives of the website marketing strategy, you can work on the remainder of the strategy. The next step is to consider who are the users? Ideally, you will have done this already for the site development plan, and can incorporate it within the marketing plan and add extra information if necessary. It should contain characteristics of the expected visitors to your site including:

- typical age range;
- typical mix of male and female;
- other key demographic information;
- parts of the world/languages spoken;
- expertise in using computers and navigating the web;
- typical interests that they may have;
- what other sites are they likely to visit.

This analysis will serve as a reminder to those involved in the marketing plan who the site is for and it is especially useful for anyone not involved in the original development plan.

Another useful activity is to research your competitors' website marketing activities – what are they doing well, what are they doing badly, how high up search engines' search results are they? Once you have gathered the relevant information, you will need to state how you will use your ideas to achieve the objectives set out in the website marketing strategy. There are a number of suggested tactics listed in *Table 9.1* and discussed in more detail in the rest of this chapter.

Site design	There are many factors to consider in designing the pages of your site to increase the number of visitors. *Section 9.2, page 142* considers this in detail.
Company literature	All company literature, letter heads, compliment slips, business cards, brochures, catalogues, e-mail signatures, and off-line advertising should carry the website address and any specific relevant pages on the website.
Search engine and directory listing	Clearly the key to getting your site known is to get your site listed as high up the search engines' search results as possible. *Section 9.3, page 143* considers this in detail.
Paid for advertising	Paid-for advertising including banner adverts must be considered in the website marketing strategy. *Section 9.4, page 147* considers paid-for advertising.
E-mail marketing	Most e-mail programs, particularly web-based ones, display messages as HTML pages and can include working hyperlinks making it very easy to drive visitors to your website from the e-mail message. E-mail is very low cost and you can reach a large number of people. E-mail newsletters (e-zines) are a good way of keeping in contact with potential customers/visitors. *Section 9.5, page 148* looks at e-mail marketing.
Information gathering	You should collect information from the people who visit your site and find out how they heard about it. It may even be worth while offering an incentive to get visitors to part with personal information for example, free software or useful documentation. Gathering information about your visitors is important as you will then be able to gauge what will encourage them to return. *Section 9.6, page 152* considers information gathering.
Visitor analysis	It is important, regardless whether people leave their details on your site or not, to automatically log all visits to your site for further analysis. *See Section 9.6, page 152* for more details.

Table 9.1: Activities that can form part of the website marketing plan

Once you have decided on the mix of marketing activities, you must implement them. As noted already, website marketing is a systematic and ongoing process, so it is important to monitor and review the success of your chosen activities, particularly those that will cost money regularly. Monitoring and reviewing should therefore be ongoing and may result in changes to the activities that you have engaged in as part of the strategy (*see Figure 9.1*).

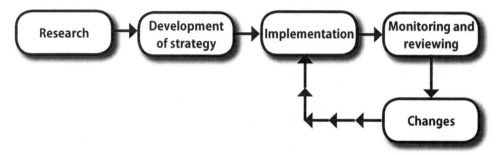

Figure 9.1: The stages in developing and implementing a website marketing strategy

9.2: Web page and site design

The design of your site is important for a number of reasons:

- the general appeal of your site will attract visitors;

- its usability will make visitors happy to use your site;

- it's adherence to web standards will make it more likely to appear properly in different browsers and be accessible; and

- how it is coded will make it more likely that the search engines will index it.

There are whole books dedicated to web page design so in this section we will just cover some of the most important things to consider.

Unless you are an experienced designer, the most important points to remember when designing a site for appeal and usability is to keep the design straightforward and be consistent in the styles that you use for text, buttons, links and layout. Also be consistent in the way that users navigate around your site, for example keep the navigation irems in the same general location on each page. Make sure that, as people navigate around your site, they can quickly find their way back to somewhere already visited. An ideal way of doing this is to implement a **breadcrumb**, which is a chronological sequence of hyperlinks to the pages visited in a site. The open directory project site **dmoz.org** is a good example of a site using a breadcrumb – when anyone browses around the dmoz site it leaves the breadcrumb along the top of the page as shown in this example:

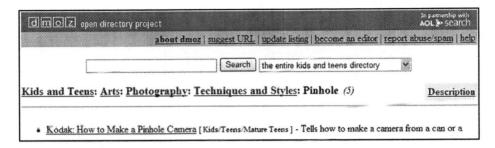

This means that the user browsed to the page 'Kids and Teens' from there they followed the link to 'Arts', then 'Photography' and so on. If the user wants to retrace their journey, all they need to do is click back along the breadcrumb.

> **TIP**
>
> The term breadcrumb comes from the story of *Hansel and Gretel* who left a trail of breadcrumbs to find their way out of a forest.

The content must be written clearly and in the style of the likely viewer (see the comments about user needs analysis, *Section 7.2, page 111*).

Although many companies and homes now have high speed Internet connections via broadband, there are still many homes connected via dial-up. Therefore, it is still important to keep the size of web pages to a minimum. A significant contribution to the size of web pages are its images it; therefore, ensure image sizes are kept to a minimum. *Section 2.6, page 23* covers the principles of image optimisation.

9.3: Search engines

Clearly, raising your website higher up in the ranking of search engines' search results is the key to getting your website known. A whole new industry has emerged to improve the ranking of websites, and note that among the legitimate businesses there are many dubious ones. It is difficult to have your site listed, but and trying to moving it up the rankings is even harder. There are several reasons for this:

- the number of sites competing to be listed;
- the secrecy of the algorithms used to list sites;
- the volume of sites already listed; and
- the design of specific elements of web pages.

There are a number of standard strategies to adopt in getting sites listed. Search engines use **spider** programs that follow links on pages and systematically analyse and index every linked page of a site. To encourage the spiders to index your pages, make sure that each page is hyperlinked to another. Having a site map with links to pages in your site and submitting these to search engines is a very useful tactic (see **www.google.com/webmasters/sitemaps/**).

It is worth noting that spiders do not like frame sets, this is because the HTML document containing the frameset information contains little else and the spider does not know what to follow (unless you have created a no-frames version as well).

Each page in a site should have a well-designed HTML **title** and **meta tags** listed in the **head** tag. For example, here is a typical head tag for this book:

```
<head>
    <title>Website Management</title>
<meta name="description" content="text book for
students covering the underpinning technology and the
principles of managing and maintaining a website." />
<meta name="keywords" content="website marketing,
management, maintenance, web servers, apache, IIS,
accessibility, usability, e-commerce, databases,
networks, ISPs, web hosting, programming" />
</head>
```

Search engines vary in how they spider and index pages, but a good general rule of thumb is that they focus on the:

- title;
- description;
- headline of page;

– in that order of importance.

The keyword `<meta>` tag is often now ignored by search engines and can be omitted. However, it is important that the 'title', 'description' and the content of the page contain the key words, but do not repeat the same keyword more than three times per tag otherwise the search engines might reject the page. Ensuring that the title right is important since it is often the text included in the listing of the page in the search engines. Therefore, the title should be a concise description of the site. Do not use titles such as 'the best site in the world' because the search engines will ignore them. **Keyword density** is the percentage of the number of times keywords are mentioned in a page compared to the total number of words. It is important to keep keyword density to no more than three percent otherwise the search engines will view your site as 'spam'. Picking the right key words is critical, they must be the same words that users of search engines are likely to use. Overture (**http://inventory.overture. com**) (*see Section 9.4, Sponsored ads, page 147*) and Google (**https://adwords. google.com/select/KeywordToolExternal**) have produced a free tool that you can use to check the words and phrases people are using in their searches that match to the subject matter of your site.

Some designers have used text the same colour as the background to try and include extra content that is aimed at search engine spiders, but not visible to the reader. However, search engines are aware of this trick and are likely to ignore your site if you use it.

Two other techniques that are used are 'doorways' and 'cloaking', but these are frowned upon by the search engines and will probably be ignored if discovered. Doorways are single page websites with very specific content to target specific searches and user profiles (e.g. under 30-year-olds), associated to a domain name that also targets specific search strings. When a user clicks on a doorway page which comes up in the search engine they are quickly redirected to the real site. A site may have multiple doorway pages each corresponding to a specific product or service or customer type. Cloaking is similar, but the process is more automated. The search engines are 'shown' a page which they index, but when users follow the link from a listing in the search engines, they are shown a different page by the web server.

Once you are happy with your site and page design and have worked on the `<title>` and `<meta>` tags, you can think about how to have your site listed in the search engines. The three biggest search engines are Google, Yahoo and MSN and they also provide the content for third-party search engines, so it makes sense to focus on these three to maximise your search engine impact. Google and MSN use spiders to automatically search through the web to find pages and sites to list, Yahoo, on the other hand, is based on a hierarchy of categories and uses humans to index everything! Many agree that the best way to get listed is to ensure your site is linked to other (reputable) sites from which the spider programs can find your site, e.g. trade association sites, blog sites, etc. If you want to submit your site to Google or MSN, you can visit these addresses:

Google
www.google.com/addurl/

MSN
http://search.msn.com/docs/submit.aspx

However, there is no guarantee that your site will be indexed. You should make sure that your site is correctly designed before submitting it because the first submission will have most impact with the search engines. Do not submit more often than every three weeks, otherwise it can be detrimental to your chances of getting listed. Yahoo, along with a number of other search engines, is a **directory**. This means that all sites included are listed under categories and subcategories, sub-subcategories and so on. To be listed in the places best for your site, you must navigate through the Yahoo category 'tree'. For instance, if you are a college wanting to offer a new course in marine science, one of the sub-categories you might want to submit it to is:

Directory > Regional > Countries > United Kingdom > Society and Culture > Environment and Nature > Education

Once you have browsed to the subcategories that you want your site listed under, select the 'Suggest a Site' link positioned at the top of the page. From here you should then be able to submit your site with relevant information.

Another important directory site is the **open directory project** at **dmoz.org**, which is the largest, most comprehensive human-edited directory on the web. It is constructed and maintained by a vast number of volunteer editors from around the world. There is evidence to indicate that some search engines, such as Google, take a great deal of notice of the sites listed by dmoz, so this is an excellent staring point if you want your site listed by the big search engines.

Table 9.2 lists the other important factors to consider when getting your site listed with search engines.

Link popularity	Due to the use of various tricks such, as doorway pages, search engines increasingly rely on **link popularity** to decide whether to list a page. Link popularity simply means how many other relevant sites have links on their pages to your pages. To improve your link popularity, encourage other sites to link to your site. Do not use link exchange programmes or Free For All (FFA) sites, as search engines will reject these and your site in the process. A good way is to approach sites that are complementary to your site and ask to be included in their pages; in exchange, you will link to theirs. A site's link popularity will increase if you have relevant and fresh content, it will also boost your site rankings in the search results (*see Content below*).
Content	Search engines like fresh content, therefore sites that are updated regularly and add new content tend to gain higher rankings in search results.
URLs, path and filenames	If possible, try and provide useful path and filenames as these are often used for search results rankings. For example, www.cardesign.co.uk/car-design-tutorial.htm will do significantly better than www.c-des.co.uk/12345.htm in searches for car design.
Click popularity	If you manage to get listed, then the number of people who click on your listing will have some bearing on how high up the search engines' search results you appear, although it's not certain how much effect this has.

**Table 9.2: Additional activities to improve
a site's listings in the search engines**

There are many web-based companies that, for a fee, will automatically submit your site to a range of search engines. The effectiveness of these services is questionable and you should proceed with caution.

9.4: Advertising

Sponsored ads

In addition to free submissions, a large number of search engines have implemented **sponsored ads** listings services. Google has a service called **Adwords (http://adwords.google.com)**, Yahoo **Sponsored Search (http://searchmarketing.yahoo.com)** (previously called Overture) and MSN **AdCenter**. These all work in roughly the same way when you sign for the service:

i)   you create one or more small advertisements using their online tools;

ii) you associate your advertisements with particular keywords that you think people are likely to use when searching for yours or similar sites;

iii) you set the **cost per click** for each of your keywords or phrases;

iv) your advertisements will start appearing alongside the normal search engine listings when your chosen keywords are used; and

v)   you only pay the cost per click when someone actual clicks on your advertisement.

Figure 9.2 shows examples of paid-for advertisements for the search term 'marine science courses' used on Google, but you would find a similar display on Yahoo and MSN. Sponsored advertising is very cost-effective, provided you have chosen your keywords carefully and targeted the advertisements correctly, since only the people you want will see your advertisements and only those attracted to the content of your advertisement will click on them.

Figure 9.2: Examples of paid for adverts on Google

When users subscribe to a sponsored ad service they can select which regions of the world they want their advertisements to appear in and which to exclude. Users also gain access to a number of free web-based tools that enable them to track and analyse the performance of their advertisements and make any necessary changes.

Banner ads are horizontal (leaderboard) or vertical (skycraper) rectangular blocks that appear on web pages and contain static or animated images. Banner ads vary in size, but are typically 500 to 700 pixels wide by 50 to 100 high and are a more expensive form of advertising than sponsored ads. In general, you pay for your banner ads to appear on sites and pages aimed at the targeted audience for your website. With banner ads, you generally pay per thousand times the advertisement is displayed, not just when it is clicked on. The effectiveness of banners ads is quite low and you should not expect a **click through rate (CTR)** of more than 0.2%.

There are a number of companies that will manage your banner advertisements campaigns. These companies have agreements with third-party sites to display their banner ads so every time a page is visited a different banner ad is displayed. Banner ads are generally more expensive than sponsored ads and only larger companies tend to use them.

If you decide to use banner ads, then it is important that the ad is designed to attract people and make them want to click on it. The basic principles of designing a banner ad are:

- always include some instruction to follow the advertisement, e.g. 'click here';

- if possible, use short engaging animations made with animated GIFs or Adobe Flash;

- give people an incentive for clicking the advertisement, e.g. 'free software'; and

- make sure the size of the banner ad in bytes is as small as possible to load quickly.

All heavily-visited sites tend to offer banner advertising and will provide contact details if you are interested in advertising with them.

9.5: E-mail marketing

E-zines are newsletters that are sent via e-mail and are an excellent way to keep in touch with your customers and visitors by regularly updating them on the latest news of your site and products. The first step in producing a successful e-zine is to build the mailing list. The best way to build the mailing list is to encourage visitors to your site and to sign up for it voluntarily. You can encourage visitors by possibly offering things such as: free software, tips or useful information, tutorials, access to reserved areas of your site, screen savers, etc. You need to make it easy for them to subscribe so do not ask for too much information up front. You must also put them at ease and ensure them that their privacy is guaranteed and that you will not share their information with anyone else (*see Data Protection Act, page 152*). It is possible to buy mailing lists, but the value of these is questionable; it is much better to develop your own list of people who have already proven their interest by visiting your site rather than use unreliable and often expensive lists. Once you have established a mailing list, it is important to maintain it. You should regularly check that all the addresses still work and remove any that do not. Ideally, you should automate the process of removing people from your list when they wish to so. You will need to add a **web page form** linked to a database somewhere on your site to collect visitor information. *Section 6.2, page 96* explains how web page forms work in detail.

Once you have your mailing list, you can start sending e-zines. Most people can now receive HTML-based e-mail, which can be made more engaging than simple text-based messages. Your e-zine should be designed to improve your customer relations and keep reminding potential customers of your products and services. You can use the e-zine to answer any questions they may have and convince them that you are a reliable organisation. You must ensure that the content of your e-zine will be interesting and useful with relevant information, product updates and, importantly, hyperlinks to pages on your website. Do not send e-zines too often, or they may annoy the recipients and keep each item of news short. *Table 9.3* includes some ideas that you should adopt when writing an e-zine.

TIPS

Here are some top tips if you plan to send an e-mail marketing letter:

- Test your e-mails over and over again before sending them to your list.
- Check that all links work when the e-zine is opened on another PC i.e. NOT the one on which you created your e-zine.
- Check any images that you have included are displayed correctly. It is all too easy to link to files or images that are stored on a local machine and that your customers will never see.
- Make your HTML files standards-compliant as this can help in getting past spam filters.

Understand your customers/viewers	You should write in the tone and language that your customers identify with, e.g. you would write in a different way for teenagers compared to IT managers.
Uniqueness of site/ product or service	What is so special about your site or product? What ever it is, it should come through in your e-zine.
Use an engaging subject line	Most people receive many e-mails a day, you must therefore ensure your subject line is engaging and will encourage them to open it (see more on avoiding spam filters below).
Personalise messages	Where you can, personalise your e-zines. There is software available for managing e-mail lists that also enables you to personalise messages.
Key information at the beginning	Ensure that you place the information that you want your customers/visitors in the first paragraph of your e-zine. They might not read the rest.
Encourage readers to act	As with banner ads, you should ask your e-zine reader to act, e.g. buy a special offer, sign up for a new service, register their interest, view more detail.
Offer an incentive	You can always offer your e-zine reader an incentive for taking action, for example a useful tip or free information.

Table 9.3: Ideas to adopt when writing an e-zine

Spam

Unwanted e-mails sent out by unscrupulous organisations are called **spam**. Spam is a huge problem and most companies and ISPs have installed sophisticated **spam filter** applications to prevent them from reaching users' mailboxes. Spam filters are a real problem for organisations wanting to send genuine e-mails to people who have consented. There are two main types of spam filter, header filters and content filters. Organisations that send spam will often fake the details in the header of an e-mail so that the sender cannot be traced. So header filters work by trying to identify fake headers. Content filters examine the title and body of the message and are programmed to look for tell-tale signs, e.g. particular words and phrases, overuse of capitals and exclamation marks. If a message passes a threshold of suspicious content, it will be blocked. For people wanting to send genuine bulk messages, spam filters pose a real problem. To prevent your messages being blocked by spam filters, avoid certain key words and phrases and not use capitalised words and exclamation marks. *Table 9.4* contains a list of commonly-used words and phrases in spam. Another technique you can adopt is to test your message out with friends' e-mail addresses against on their spam filters.

Hidden	Stop or stops	100% Satisfied
4U	50% Off!	Accept credit cards
Act now!	Additional income	All natural
All new	Amazing	Apply online
As seen on...	Avoid bankruptcy	Best price
Billing address	Buy direct	Call free
Call now!	Can't live without	Cash
Cash bonus	Casino	Cents on the dollar
Click here	Collect	Compare
Consolidate your debt	Credit	Discount!
Do it today	Don't delete	Double your income
Earn $	Easy terms	Eliminate debt
For free	Free leads	Free website
Free!	Full refund	Get paid
Give it away	Great offer	Guarantee, guaranteed
Increase sales	Increase traffic	Information you requested
Join millions	Loans	Lose weight
Meet singles	Million dollars	Mlm
Multi level marketing	No cost, no fees	No gimmicks
No hidden costs	No-obligation	Offer
One time	Online marketing	Online pharmacy
Opportunity	Order now	Please read
Pre-approved	Promise you	Removes
Reverses aging	Risk free	Satisfaction guaranteed
Save $	Save up to	Search engine listings
Search engines	See for yourself	Serious cash
Sex	Special promotion	Special offers
Subscribe	Time limited	Unsecured debt or credit
Urgent	Vacation	Viagra
Visit our website	While supplies last	Why pay more?
Win	Winner	Work at home
You're a winner!		

Table 9.4: Words and phrases used to identify spam

There are legal issues that govern what you can do with mailing lists and sending e-mails. In the European Union, the *Privacy and Electronic Communications (EC Directive) Regulations 2003* cover unsolicited direct marketing sent by electronic means, including e-mail. Organisations can only send unsolicited marketing by e-mail to individuals where the individual has specifically requested it, i.e. they have opted in. There are three exceptions to this rule:

1. the organisation obtained the details in the course of a sale or the negotiations for a sale of a product or service;

2. the messages are only marketing similar products or services; and

3. the individual is given a simple opportunity to opt-out when their details are collected and are given an opportunity to opt out of all future messages.

Individuals can opt out of receiving marketing at any time by contacting the organisation directly and they must comply with any opt out requests promptly. Businesses are exempt from this rule and it only covers mail that originates from within the EU. If you collect personal information (i.e. you are defined as an 'information controller') that includes e-mail addresses, then the *1998 Data Protection Act* requires that you register with the **Information Commissioners' Office (www.ico.gov.uk)** and that you apply the **eight enforceable principles** to the data you collect. Data must be:

- fairly and lawfully processed;

- processed for limited purposes;

- adequate, relevant and not excessive;

- accurate and up to date;

- not kept longer than necessary;

- processed in accordance with the individual's rights;

- secure; and

- not transferred to countries outside the European Economic area, unless there is adequate protection.

9.6: Information gathering, analysis and review

The final stage in the marketing strategy is monitoring and reviewing its success. With respect to website marketing, this means answering the following questions:

- How many people have visited the site over particular periods?

- What times of day did they visit?

- What are the demographics of people who have visited the site?

- From which regions of the world are your visitors?

- How did they discover your site (e.g. search engine, printed material, etc.)?

- Which sites were your visitors on before yours, i.e. what link did they follow to get to your site?

- What pages have been viewed and what is the visit rate?

- If a visitor came from a search engine link, which words and phrases were used?

- If you are selling something, what is the ratio of visitors to buyers, i.e. the conversion rate?

- What types and versions of browsers, operating systems, screen resolutions and colour depths are being used by people to access your site?

- What is the percentage of return visitors to new visitors?

Armed with this information you can make informed decisions about which marketing activities are working and those that are not, and therefore what needs changing. This information also helps you to optimise the structure and design of your site.

There are several applications available that enable you to monitor your website performance. One of the best of these is **Google Analytics** (**www.google. com/analytics**), which is free and enables you track the detailed performance of your site. To use Google Analytics you need to create a Google account, insert a small piece of code into each page of your site and sign up for Google Analytics. *Figure 9.3* shows a typical screen of the marketing summary for **www. pembrokeshire.ac.uk** from Google Analytics, which shows that 17% of visitors typed the address in directly, 12% found the site from a Google search and the number of people finding the site from MSN has increased dramatically since it was submitted to the search engine.

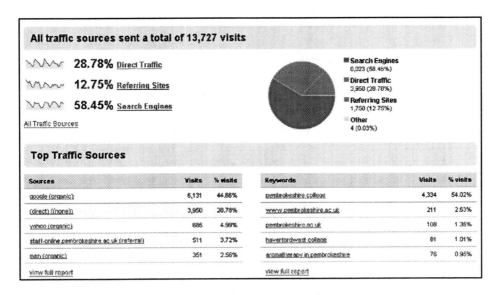

Figure 9.3: Summary table from Google Analytics

9.7: Chapter summary

Website marketing is part of the overall marketing activities of a company. However, for many companies, particularly those operating online, it is the crucial component. Website marketing starts with setting objectives. Then deciding on a range of activities and tactics to realise those objectives, the results of any activity should be monitored and any necessary changes made. Key website marketing activities include:

- optimising website and page design for usability and search engine acceptance;
- search engine submission;
- paid-for sponsored advertising and banner advertising; and
- e-mail marketing.

Monitoring the effectiveness of website marketing requires setting up server-based applications to log website usage. It is important to analyse the data from monitoring the website and make any changes to the site and website marketing tactics.

9.8: Example questions

1. The marketing manager is putting together a marketing plan for a small charity. He has already drafted the objectives of the strategy. As a web master what activities can you suggest that should be included to promote the website and its services?

2. The same marketing manager is taken by the idea of starting an e-zine for all the charities' volunteers, staff and donors. What are the issues associated with producing and circulating an e-zine that you would outline?

9.9: Example answers

1. The first thing you should ask is to see a copy of the draft marketing strategy. Ask what are its objectives and what is the budget? Assuming there is a budget, you can explain the different ways in which the objectives could be met and then go into some detail about each option. Start by outlining the activities that you think are the least costly such as the importance of optimising the design of the charity website for the benefit of the search engines. Explain how difficult it is to get listed in the search engines. You could mention the importance of usability and designing the site for the specific kinds of people the marketing manager wants to attract. Then you might discuss the options of paid-for advertising and its relative effectiveness, perhaps explaining that sponsored listings are the most cost-effective form of advertising because you only pay when someone clicks on one of your listings. Finally, explain that the charity needs to monitor website usage, using a tool, such as Google Analytics, together with some training in its use for the marketing team. You might want to explain the different reports that can be obtained from monitoring website usage.

2. Explain the need to develop a good mailing list first and, although the charity has its databases of volunteers, workers and donors, it will need to obtain permission from anyone listed on their existing databases to e-mail them. You might want to reinforce this point by outlining the legal position with regard to sending e-mails to people. You might say in your answer that you would ask the marketing manager whether he wants three e-zines for the three types of people or one combined since this will affect the content of the e-zine and the style of writing. You could suggest that the purpose of an e-zine for volunteers will be to encourage them to volunteer more often, for donors to give more and more frequently and for staff to keep them updated on developments in the charity and the wider environment. You might want to give the marketing manager some advice on how to write an e-zine based on all the points mentioned in *Section 9.5, page 148*. Close by mentioning the problem of spam filters and the legitimate ways they can be avoided.

9.10: Further reading and research

Websites

Add the number in square brackets to **www.bookref.net/lpwm** for the most up to date web link, for example www.bookref.net/lpwm0110

www.google.com/intl/az/webmasters/guidelines.html – guidelines from Google on website design. **[0901]**

www.apromotionguide.com – website promotion guide. **[0902]**

www.webmasterresources.com – website promotion guide. **[0903]**

www.traffic4me.com – more ideas on website marketing. **[0904]**

Chapter 10

E-COMMERCE AND OTHER WEB-BASED APPLICATIONS

Chapter overview

This chapter looks primarily at how web-based online shops work and other common web applications.

Learning outcomes

After studying this chapter and by answering the examples at the end of the chapter (*see page 166*), you should be able to achieve these outcomes:

Outcome 1: Outline the main principles of web-based e-commerce.

Outcome 2: Develop a rudimentary requirement specification for an online shop.

Outcome 3: Outline the main web-based applications.

How will you be assessed on this?

Coursework assessment on this topic will probably expect you to develop a requirements specification for an online shop. Exam-based assessments might ask you to explain how online shops work or you might be given a hypothetical situation and asked to consider how you would go about designing an online shop.

10.1: Introduction to e-commerce

E-commerce is either carried out business-to-customer, referred to as **B2C**, or business-to-business, referred to as **B2B**. B2B e-commerce is more complex than B2C involving negotiations over prices, delivery and product specifications with the business relationships extending over long periods of time. In contrast, B2C e-commerce transactions are discrete, there are no negotiations since prices are fixed and a sale is completed during one visit to a website. B2C e-commerce in the context of the web generally means an **online shop** or store. Below are the steps in which a typical online shop operates:

1. users browse and search for services or products for sale using the site's search tools;

2. users choose items to be purchased and add them to their shopping basket. Shopping baskets are an important element of online shops that remember which items the user wishes to purchase;

3. users can view their shopping basket at any time and modify or delete its contents;

4. once users have finished selecting their goods they are then invited to register and store their details (Name address, delivery address, etc.) with the online shop or log in if they have previously registered. Sometimes registration is not required and the user can move to step 6) without storing their details;

5. users enter/retrieve their delivery details;

6. users enter/retrieve payment details, once they have finished shopping; and finally,

7. the order is confirmed on the final submit button.

The details of returning users are automatically retrieved from the database. Steps 5–7 are usually undertaken using a secure HTTPS connection (*see Section 3.4, page 42* for an explanation of HTTPS) to ensure privacy. Users will receive an e-mail confirming the order.

Typically, online shops are built using a database management system (*see Section 6.3, page 102*) connected to the web server that can store details and prices of products and services, details of users and contents of shopping baskets.

There are a number of methods of storing the contents of a shopping basket. When someone enters an online shop, the shopping site application creates a new shopping basket record with a unique session variable plus the IP address of the visitor. In some systems, this record is written to a database on the web server, in some, it is stored in a cookie and some systems use both methods. When a visitor clicks an 'add to basket' button, the details of the chosen item are added to the shopping basket record, either the database on the server, the cookie on the visitors' computer or both. Some shopping basket applications just use JavaScript and store the shopping basket contents in arrays; however, the basket contents are lost if the browser is accidentally closed or the user moves away from the online shop.

When visitors are ready to pay, their details are also associated with the shopping basket. As noted in step 4 above, visitor details are either retrieved from the database when the visitor logs-in or entered there and then. Some online shops also store the details of visitors in cookies on the visitors' computers so that they can be retrieved by the online shop application if visitors return for more shopping. Most online shops store the details of products and services, prices and users in a database (see Section 6.3, page 102) connected to the web server.

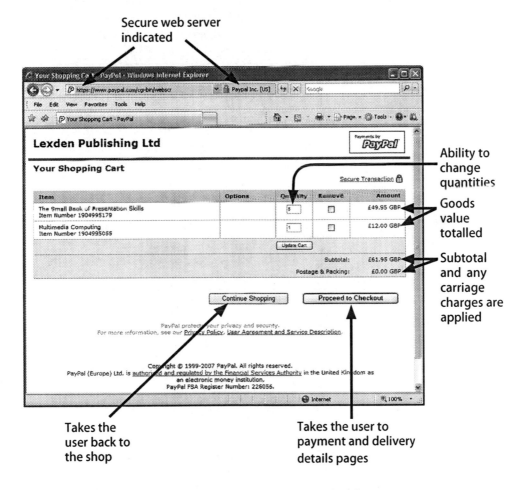

Figure 10.1: Typical shopping basket features

Online payments require setting up a connection to a **payment service provider (PSP),** which provides a secure mechanism for customers to enter their payment details from the online store and then arrange for the payment to be debited from the customers account. Online payments also require a shop owner to set up a web **merchant bank account** into which the PSP deposits the money. A merchant bank account is simply a bank account designated by banks for trading use.

Anyone operating an online shop must be aware of the legislation and regulations of trading online. In the UK, there are three pieces of legislation governing trading online:

Data Protection Act 1998	This Act deals with the issues of storing personal information and means you must conform to the eight principles of data protection.
Consumer Protection (Distance Selling) Regulations 2000	These regulations require traders to give customers specified information before they order, for example company name and address. Traders are also required to send the buyer a confirmation and give them a 'cooling off period'. An important part of this is allowing customers to go back and correct mistakes.
Electronic Commerce Regulations 2002	These regulations define what information you must share with your customer and also that they must be able to print off any contractual details.

10.2: Designing an online shop

When a business sets up an online shop it needs to have a clear idea of:

- it's business requirements (e.g. payment methods, terms and conditions, any discount structures, etc.); and

- the functionality, i.e. how it expects its customers will want to use the system.

Once these facts have been gathered they can be formalised in a **requirements specification.** The requirements specification can be used to describe precisely to web development companies what the business wants. This section presents a simple approach to developing a requirements specification for an online shop. For a more detailed coverage of web page design, refer to *Further reading and research, page 167.* In the first instance, the competitor sites should be evaluated to see what features are good and bad. A straightforward way to evaluate a website is to use the **inspection method** with a prescribed list of criteria. Typical criteria that could be used include:

- readability;
- ease of navigation;
- match of site structure to user needs;
- match of functionality to user needs;
- match of functionality to the business model needs;
- quality of layout;
- good site features;
- bad site features.

Once a set of criteria has been drawn up it is possible to rate and make notes of each competitor website against each criterion. Following this exercise, it is possible to draw up a clearer list of requirements.

It is important when designing an online shop to have a clear idea who will use the shop and how it will be used. A useful way to achieve this is to produce **user scenarios**, as explained in *Section 7.2, page 111*.

Flowcharts can also encapsulate the key interactions users will have with the site, as covered in *Section 7.2, page 111*. *Figure 10.2* is an outline of a flowchart that describes the process of a simple search for an item of clothing on an online shop. The small codes in each element, such as 's1' refer to a **storyboard** of that page.

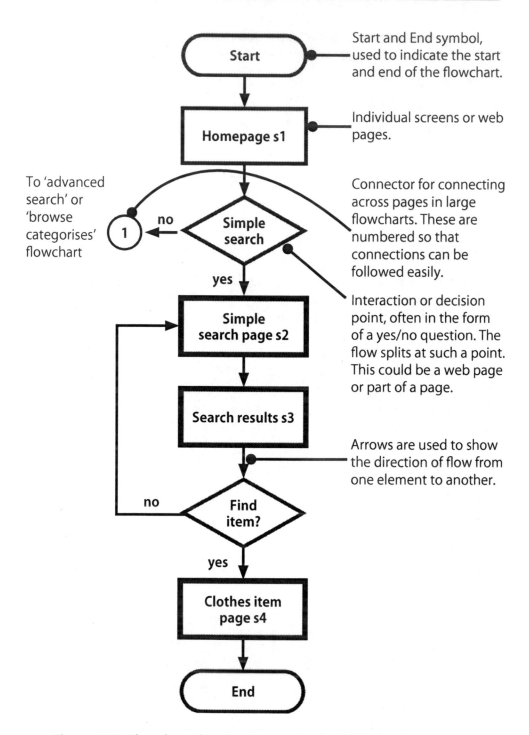

Figure 10.2: Flowchart showing the sequence of actions of a customer performing a simple search in an online shop

Now that we have a good idea how the shop will be used the structure of the online shop needs to be considered. *Figure 10.3* shows a typical **structure chart** of the online shop (*see Section 7.2, page 111* for details on structure charts).

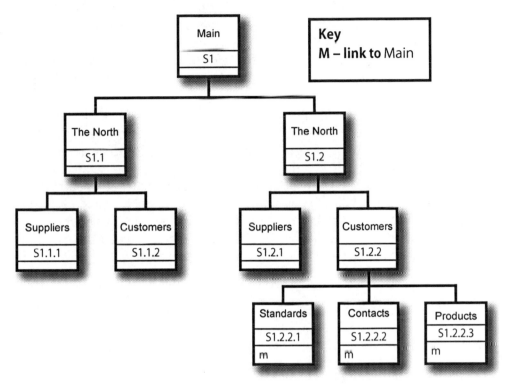

Figure 10.3: A simple structure chart

Structure charts can become unwieldy if too much detail is included, for instance suppose you wanted a direct link from the 'Products' node to the main page it would be indicated as a line joining the two. This is OK for one link, but when there are many cross links it starts to look a mess. A simple solution is to introduce a coding system so that when a node links back to the 'Main' page you place an 'M' in the rectangle as shown in *Figure 10.3 above*.

The requirements specification can now be compiled from the evaluation of competitor websites, the user scenarios, flowcharts and structure charts.

10.4: Building an online shop

Once you have agreed on the page design and layout and site structure, it is time to build your site and find somewhere to host it. Generally, online shop sites consist of two components:

- a normal website; and

- an online shop facility.

Sites vary in the relative size of these two components, for some sites the online shop is just a small addition to a large site of interesting content, but some sites are online shops only.

The normal website component can be built in the conventional way, based on the material covered elsewhere in this book. *Chapter 2, pages 13–34*, explains the technology that should be employed to build the pages optimally, *Chapter 5, pages 75–92* and *Chapter 6, pages 93–107* show how server-side programming and databases are used to build websites. *Section 8.3, page 128* explains the advantages of using a Content Management System to build and maintain websites.

There are now many companies and ISPs offering 'off-the-shelf' online shop facilities and solutions that can be tailored to the needs of most people's requirements. Therefore, unless the goods to be sold are complex, an 'off-the-shelf' solution should be sort rather than building a facility from scratch. **www. easywebstore.co.uk** is a typical example of a company that enables customers to build online shops without having any technical expertise. Anyone wishing to use an off-the-shelf online shop facility should spend time comparing the various packages available and the levels of service guaranteed from ISPs and web hosting companies. *Section 4.2, page 60* and *Section 4.3, page 66* cover these in detail.

10.5: Other applications

In this section, we review some of the more widely known and successful web-based applications and businesses that have evolved in recent years.

Portal and member sites

Portals and member sites are websites dedicated to a particular subject area or interest such as pets, weddings, travelling or even shopping. Portals contain material, documents and links to other sites that are relevant to the subject area of the portal. Most portals enable visitors to register so that the information the portal presents is personalised. Portals trade by charging for advertising space or taking a small commission for each time a visitor is referred from the portal site to another site. A good example is **www.lovemypets.com**.

Online newspapers and magazines

Online newspapers are generally the online equivalent of physical newspapers. The differences between them are:

- articles remain available for longer periods of time, even years;
- visitors can search for news items;
- wider coverage of news and items of interest;
- online store integrated with site;
- no fee for viewing, but newspapers trade by charging for advertising space.

A good example is the Guardian online **www.guardian.co.uk**.

Online banking

Online banking is simply the migration of a traditional bank's services to a web-based format. Some banks only exist online and therefore make their money by charging for traditional banking services delivered via the web. Online banking has the advantage over traditional banking in that customers can view and manage their account or view previous statements whenever they wish (provided they have a connection to the web).

A good example of an online bank is Smile (**www.smile.co.uk**), part of the Co-operative Bank.

Auction sites

Auction sites enable people to buy or sell items in much the same way as traditional bricks and mortar auction rooms. Sellers can put the details of items they want to sell on the auction site by providing a description and a photo (if they wish), a specified starting bid price, an optional reserve price and a designated period that the item in which bids can be placed . Buyers can browse or search for items and read the descriptions and view the images. If they want to try and win that item, they can register a 'bid' to the maximum price they are willing to pay against that item. At a designated time for that item's auction to end the highest bidder wins.

Payments are managed through the auction site and it is the responsibility of the seller to arrange delivery of the goods. The auction site makes its money by charging a listing price and commission from the seller of every successful auction.

The most popular auction site is **www.ebay.com**.

Share dealing

People who want to buy or sell shares can now do so online. They can check on the current value of their own portfolio of shares, check the prices of any company or stock they are interested in and buy and sell shares. Online stockbrokers make their money by charging commissions on each transaction. Online share dealing offers customers more control over their business than traditional share dealing since online sites include applications for tracking, comparing and analysing stocks, instant updates on share values that a traditional broker could not offer.

www.iii.co.uk is a good example of a share dealing site.

Gambling

Gambling websites offer customers online casinos, live Internet roulette, sports betting, bingo, lotteries, card games and even slot machines. Gambling sites make their money in the same way traditional gambling organisations do. Online gambling is an enormous worldwide market and also becoming a serious problem for gambling addiction, as anyone can gamble any time of day or night without visiting a live casino or betting shop.

Delivery companies

Delivery companies have extended their operations to an online format. Delivery websites enable customers to register and pay for items to be collected and delivered; customers can then check the status of their delivery online. Delivery companies make their money by charging for their services.

A good example of a delivery company online is **www.parceline.com**.

Search engines

Search engines are a key feature of the web and are quite often the starting point of most web browsing. Search engine companies have evolved into big businesses by charging for advertising and the listing of sites. The largest search engine, Google, is worth about £70 billion, it employees about 2,000 people and about 82 million users visit every month.

> **TIP**
>
> Your tutor may set a general question about website design or management. If you can base your answer on a specific example of a website application as laid out in this section, it will make your answer more convincing. Find your own real example of each of the application types listed here so that you can refer to them in your work.

10.6: Example questions

1. As a web design consultant you have been asked to examine the website of an unsuccessful online shop selling computer games and suggest improvements to the site. What steps would you take to improve this site?

2. What issues need to be taken into account when building an online shop and then trading online?

10.7: Example answers

1. This is a question about the design of online shops so you can start by going through the design stages covered in *Section 10.2, page 160*:

    - evaluate competitor sites and the existing site using the same evaluation criteria and draw up a list of needs and features and elements that are not working;

    - develop user scenarios for the major ways in which the online shop will be used;

    - develop flowcharts based on the user scenarios; and

    - produce structure charts to describe what the structure of the failed online shop should be.

Having outlined these stages you can then explain that it would now be possible to draw up a clearer requirements specification and then redesign the site with this to guide you. Good answers might give examples when describing each of the design stages.

2. To answer this question you can refer to *Section 10.4, page 163* and explain that an online shop consists of two components, the conventional website and the online shop with shopping basket and checkout. The design of the website component will follow the normal development path and here you could mention all the factors that need to be taken into account (e.g. accessibility). The design of the online shop component will depend on the complexity of the product. If it is a fairly straightforward product with only a few parameters to select per stock item then an 'off-the-shelf' solution can be used. If the product is very complex and requires significant input from the customers to define the product (e.g. buying a new car online), then a tailor-made solution is possible. You can make the point that most off-the-shelf solutions can be 'tweaked' to suit the needs of individual clients. You might want to mention the legislative requirements that an online shop must abide by and that these must be built into the design.

10.8: Further reading and research

Books

Cunliffe, D. and Elliott, G. (2005) *Multimedia Computing*, Lexden Publishing: Colchester.

Websites

Add the number in square brackets to **www.bookref.net/lpwm** for the most up to date web link, for example www.bookref.net/lpwm0110

www.businesslink.gov.uk – the businesslink site is run by the UK Government that provides advice to businesses and has a good section on e-commerce. [1001]

www.dti.gov.uk/consumers/buying-selling/distance-selling/index.html – advice on UK legislation governing online trading. [1002]

www.fasthosts.co.uk – is an example of an ISP offering special packages to anyone wanting to create an online e-commerce website. [1003]

www.easywebstore.co.uk – is a company providing easy-to-build online shops [1004].

Chapter 11

ACCESSIBILITY AND USABILITY

Chapter overview

This chapter briefly summarises the current legislation of accessible and usable web pages, presents the most generic guidelines and then explains how they are employed.

Learning outcomes

After studying this chapter and answering the example questions at the end of the chapter (see page 178), you should be able to achieve these outcomes:

Outcome 1: Describe the main elements of accessibility and usability.

Outcome 2: Apply the principles of accessibility and usability.

How will you be assessed on this?

Accessibility is more likely to be included as a question or part of a question in an exam. It is also likely to be a criterion of assessment in coursework where the tutor would expect you to explain in what ways you have taken into account any issues related to accessibility.

11.1: Legal requirements

Governments around the world have been introducing laws to prevent discrimination against disability at work and many of them also apply to websites. In the United States, there are several laws governing disability discrimination; however, *section 508 of the 1973 Rehabilitation Act amended in 1998* is the key one for web access. The law requires government agencies to ensure that government information on the web is accessible to employees and members of the public with disabilities, but the act does not apply to private companies. In the United States, laws on accessibility are enforced by the Accessibility Board.

In the UK, the *Disability Discrimination Act (DDA) 1995* and the *Special Educational Needs and Disability Act (SENDA) 2001* have made it unlawful for any institution in the UK to discriminate against people with disabilities for reasons associated with their disability. This includes those who are blind or have visual impairments, are deaf or hard of hearing, have medical conditions or mental health problems, language or cognitive disabilities and people with dyslexia. The legislation imposes obligations on the provider to make 'reasonable adjustments' to ensure that a person with a disability will not be placed at a disadvantage because of that disability and this requirement applies to websites. In the UK, the law is enforced by the *Disability Rights Commission.*

A disabled person can make a claim against a company if their website makes it impossible or unreasonably difficult to access information and services. If the company has not made reasonable adjustments and cannot show that this failure is justified, then it may be liable under the *DDA* or *SENDA*, and may have to pay compensation and be ordered by a court to change its site. So far, these new laws have not been tested in court. However, similar legislation exists in Australia where a successful case was brought against the Sydney Olympics Committee when it failed to make changes to its website when challenged by a blind person and had to pay $20,000 compensation and make reasonable changes. Details of this case can be found in *Further reading and research, page 179.*

Accessibility, in terms of web pages or sites, means that they can be navigated and read by everyone of the target audience language. Accessibility is usually associated with the disabled because this group is most likely to be disadvantaged if its principles are not implemented. There are a wide range of definitions of accessibility published, but until some cases have been brought to court, the legal requirements in the UK will remain uncertain.

Closely related to accessibility is the concept of **usability**. Usability is simply a measure of how easy it is to use an interface such as a web page in a browser. A web page that is highly usable will generally also be more accessible, but a page that has just been designed to comply with accessibility guidelines may not be highly usable. There are no legal requirements that websites should be usable, but if they are required to be accessible, then designing them to be usable makes sense.

11.2: Guidelines on accessibility and usability

There are many **accessibility guidelines**, **checklists** and tips, but the key ones to observe are:

- **W3C Web Content Accessibility Guidelines 1.0 (WCAG)**;

- **IBM Web Accessibility Checklist**;

- **Disability Rights Commission Good practice guide**; and

- **TechDis Web Accessibility and Usability Resource**.

The WCAGs are generally seen as the most important accessibility guidelines. The W3C have produced a draft of WCAG 2.0, which defines four principles of designing for accessibility, and makes a useful 'rules of thumb' that can be remembered as **POUR:**

Perceivable	content must be **perceivable** to each user, i.e. all users must be able to 'take in' all aspects of the website.
Operable	user interface components in the content must be **operable** by the user, i.e. all users must be able to use all aspects of the site.
Understandable	content and controls must be **understandable** to each user.
Robust	content should be **robust** enough to work with current and future technologies (including assistive technologies), e.g. on a PC monitor and PDA.

Table 11.1 on the following pages summarises the main factors that all these guidelines and checklists share.

Factor	Guideline Summary
General design and structure	• Separate the site structure from the presentation, i.e. use XHTML (eXtensible Hypertext Mark-up Language) to define the structure of the site and CSS (Cascading Style Sheets) to control the visual presentation and layout of the information. • Analyse the content of the site and define the hierarchical structure of the information right down to paragraph level before designing the visual presentation of the site. • Design for device independence.
Context and orientation	• Provide descriptive information about the site structure, how to use the navigation, and where to find the main menu information etc. early on in the design. • Provide a short description of the page layout on each page. • Provide a short descriptive preview of the page contents on each page. • Provide text/audible warnings if an action by the user will cause a new browser window to open.
Layout	• Apply the same page layout consistently throughout the site. • Use a layout that is simple, clear and free from clutter.
Navigation mechanism and links	• Provide a concise navigation mechanism that allows access to all site material. The navigation should be separate from and not affected by the main area content. • The navigation structure should be clear, simple, logical and consistent. • Where the main content material requires scrolling, provide preview links at the beginning of the information to allow the user to jump to their point of interest on the page. • Avoid using too many hyperlinks within one line of text. • Text hyperlinks should make sense when read out of context.
Colour	• Never code information using just colour alone. • Always make sure that there is high contrast between the background colour and the colour of the text and images displayed against it.

Factor	Guideline Summary
Text	• Ideally, present the text in a single column.
	• Use style sheets to allow the user full customisation of font styles, sizes and colours.
	• Use a sans serif font style that is clear and easy to read on screen.
	• Don't use font sizes that are too small to read comfortably under normal conditions.
	• Avoid using graphic images for the presentation of textual information.
	• Choose a text colour that contrasts well with the background, e.g. black or dark text on a pale background or white text on a dark background. In either case the background should be plain without pattern or imagery.
	• Split the text into manageable 'chunks' for readability.
	• Edit the text content for maximum readability.
	• When dealing with lists of information, rather than using text bullets or text numbers, use the correct HTML tags, i.e. `<ul>` and `<li>`, etc. for bullets and `<ol>` and `<li>` for numbers. Include a full stop at the end of each item on the list as an indication to screen readers that it has reached the end of each item.
	• Use appropriate punctuation throughout the text content and always include full stops at the end of sentences.
	• Avoid the underlining of text, as is the practice in denoting hyperlinks.
	• Where a 'text only' version is used as a substitute for the inaccessible elements of e-learning sites, make sure that there are procedures in place to ensure that this text content is always updated/amended alongside the main site content.

Factor	Guideline Summary
Images	• Any images used must be of the best achievable quality when optimised for web resolution. • Limit the number of images included on each web page. • Using the `<alt>` tag, provide 'alt-text' (alternative text) for all static images. • For images such as graphs or charts where longer descriptions are necessary, use the `<longdesc>` (long description) tag or the D link (description tag).
Tables	• Provide a short description as a preview of the tabular data if this would help the visually-impaired user in the understanding of the information. • Use coding to ensure that information in data cells can be easily related to column and row headings when read by a screen reader. • CSS-positioning is preferable to the `<table>` tag for creating tables.
Audio	• Supplement important auditory material with captioning or a text transcription. • Make the user aware of the type of information that is being conveyed. • If sound is used is should be of good quality to ensure maximum clarity. • A volume control should be available to allow users to make individual adjustments. • Where audio is used to accompany visual material, it should be synchronised to run appropriately alongside the visual information. • The user should have the choice of listening to the audio, reading the captioning or both.
Video	• Provide captioning, a written transcript, an audio transcript or a text description of what is happening in the video (e.g. using the 'D' (description) link).
Multimedia	• Provide a transcript or description of important multimedia content and make the distinction clear to the user. • Provide descriptive or complementary audio tracks for multimedia.

Table 11.1: Synthesis of all accessibility guidelines and checklists

Like the accessibility guidelines, there are many **usability guidelines** available for developers to consider when designing web pages. Some of the guidelines focus on HTML, some are more general in nature. The most generic set of guidelines are produced by the United States Department of Health and Human Services and are summarised in *Table 11.2* (the full details can be found in the references at the end of the chapter).

Factor	Guideline Summary
Design considerations	• Place important information at the top of the page • Reduce users' workload • Be consistent • Provide feedback to users • Include logos on every page • Limit maximum page size • Limit use of frames
Content/content organisation	• Establish level of importance of information • Provide useful content • Put important information at top of hierarchy • Use short sentence/paragraph lengths • Provide printing options • Provide page titles • Use well-designed headings
Page layout	• Align page elements • Establish level of importance page structure • Be consistent • Reduce unused space • Put important information at top of page • Format for efficient viewing • Use short pages where possible
Font/text size	• Use readable font sizes • Use familiar fonts
Reading and eye scanning	• 55 characters a line is easier to read • Support quick scanning of page • Use linked pages rather than scrolling

Factor	Guideline Summary
Links	• Position important links higher up page • Show links clearly • Indicate internal vs. external links • Use descriptive link labels • Use text links • Avoid mouseovers • Repeat text links in page in different ways • Show used links
Graphics	• Use graphics that enhance content not otherwise • Avoid using graphics as links • Avoid graphics on search pages
Searching	• Consider if adding a search facility really helps • Make it clear what a search facility searches • Make pages easy to scan quickly by eye
Navigation	• Keep navigation aids consistent • Use text-based navigation aids • Group navigation elements
Software/ hardware	• Design for connection speeds of 56kbs • Create web pages that load quickly • Consider monitor size • Consider users' screen resolution • Design for full or partial screen viewing

Table 11.2: Usability guidelines from US Department of Health and Human Services

There is a surprising amount of overlap between accessibility and usability guidelines, which should mean that, if a page is designed to be truly accessible, it will also be more usable. However, the converse is not true since there are some requirements of accessibility like using the `ALT` attribute to describe an HTML tag that are not needed to make a page usable.

11.3: Evaluating and validating accessibility

After designing web pages with the accessibility and usability guidelines, it is important to test or evaluate the web pages to ensure that they are accessible and usable. One approach is to use **automated validators** which can verify that the code in your pages (e.g., HTML, CSS) is correct. Correct coding will help eliminate a number of accessibility problems since browsers can process well-formed web pages properly. There are several automated validators available including the W3C tools for validating HTML and CSS (*see Further reading and resources, page 179* for details). To validate some of the key accessibility features in a web page's code you can use an automated validator such as **Bobby** (*see Further reading and resources, page 179*) that checks a web page against the W3C accessibility guidelines and produces a list of problems.

A second approach is to conduct an evaluation of the web pages manually by checking through the web page with a checklist to hand. **User scenarios** (*see Section 7.2, page 111*) could be produced, where several different situations of use are formulated, e.g. using a website for different purposes, using different browsers, using people with different kinds of disability and different types of computers and hardware. The idea behind user scenarios is to identify genuine problems from genuine user interactions. Ideally, at least one disabled person and, preferably, a range of people with varying disabilities can be employed to carry out this task. Each item on the checklist is evaluated as each user scenario is followed. WCAG 1.0 refers to levels of **conformance** to the guidelines, so it is a good idea to base the checklist on at least the WCAG guidelines.

Once the accessibility problems have been identified developers can use **repair tools** to help fix the problems. There are many repair tools depending on the problem so, for example, there are tools for Microsoft PowerPoint, Apple QuickTime and for the more common coding problems such as missing **ALT** attributes. Developers can also address accessibility problems through a redesign of the site using the techniques outlined in *Chapter 7, pages 109–123*, but placing a particular emphasis on accessibility.

People with particular disabilities will often use **assistive technology**, i.e. tools to help make interacting with a computer and websites easier. Assistive technology includes screen readers – tools that scan computer screens and, as the focus of attention moves around the page, the screen reader audio says what text is found at that point. Other assistive technology includes specialised input and output devices such large tracker balls, screen magnifiers, text-only browsers, Braille browsers and voice-activated browsers. Web pages should, therefore, also be evaluated using a range of commonly used assistive technologies.

11.4: Chapter summary

Accessibility and usability are essential requirements for websites because of:

- legislation; and

- simply to make sites as easy to use as possible for the maximum number of people.

There are many guidelines available for designing accessible and usable websites, which are synthesised into one list in this chapter (*see page 172–174*). All sites should be evaluated to check they are accessible and usable in a systematic way, ideally involving a number of disabled people in the evaluation process. Any problems identified should be rectified. There are some automated accessibility and usability checking utilities available that should be used, but bear in mind that they are to some extent limited and their output requires interpretation. Designers should be aware of the range of assistive technology that disabled people may utilise in browsing the web.

11.5: Example questions

1. What legal requirements are associated with the accessibility of websites?

2. What do you think are the key accessibility requirements of a website?

3. Imagine you work for a college or university as a web developer. You have been asked to review the accessibility of your institute's website. How would you go about this work and what do you think you need to take into account?

11.6: Example answers

1. This is a straightforward question that is simply asking what you know about accessibility legislation? You can base most of you answer on *Section 11.1, page 170* of this chapter. For a good answer include details from the case against the Sydney Olympics Committee. You should explain what the laws are (*DDA* and *SENDA, see Section 11.1, page 170*), what they imply and what happens when a user challenges the accessibility of a site. A good answer should also explain that, although there are many definitions of accessibility, the meaning has not been tested in a UK court of law to determine the precise legal boundaries.

2. You can start this question by mentioning the various guidelines available and, in particular, the WCAG 1.0 guidelines. The four principles of the WCAG 2.0 provide overarching 'rules of thumb' against which all websites can be assessed, e.g. 'Are all elements perceivable?, If not why not?' It is probably worth mentioning a few guidelines for each element of a web page design:

- design and structure
- layout
- navigation
- colour

- tables
- text
- images
- audio, video and multimedia

Usability should be mentioned, and also the differences and similarities between usability and accessibility.

3. This question is about:

    - the process of applying usability and accessibility evaluate techniques; and

    - redesigning a site with reference to accessibility.

    You should discuss how you would apply the evaluation techniques covered in *Section 11.3, page 177*, i.e. apply automated validators and then undertake a systematic review of the existing site using something like user scenarios and a checklist. In compiling your checklist you should refer to the various sets of guidelines and how you would draw from these to produce each item in the checklist. Once any problems and non-conformance issues have been identified, you can discuss how you would go about redesigning the site mentioning some of the techniques and design processes covered in *Chapter 7, pages 109–123*.

11.7: Further reading and research

Websites

Add the number in square brackets to **www.bookref.net/lpwm** for the most up to date web link, for example www.bookref.net/lpwm0110

www.drc-gb.org – Disability Rights Commission. [1101]

www.drc-gb.org/library/website_accessibility_guidance/pas_78.aspx – Disability Rights Commission good practice guide. [1102]

www.w3.org/WAI/GL/WCAG20/ – W3C content accessibility guidelines 2.0. [1103]

www-03.ibm.com/able/guidelines/web/accessweb.html – IBM web accessibility checklist. [1104]

www.techdis.ac.uk/seven/precepts.html – TechDis web accessibility and usability resource. [1105]

www.w3.org/TR/WAI-WEBCONTENT/full-checklist.html – W3C accessibility guidelines checklist. [1106]

http://bobby.watchfire.com/bobby/html/en/index.jsp – Bobby (automated accessibility validator). [1107]

www.tomw.net.au/2001/bat2001.html – details of case brought against Sydney Olympic Committee. [1108]

INDEX

Also from Lexden Publishing:

Title	Author	ISBN
Computer Systems Architecture	R Newman, E Gaura, D Hibbs	978-1-903337-07-0
Computer Networks (2nd Edition)	P Irving	978-1904995-08-X
Databases	R Warrender	978-1-903337-08-0
Get On Up With Java	R Picking	978-1904995-18-0
JavaScript: Creating Dynamic Web Pages	E Gandy, S Stobart	978-1904995-07-4
Multimedia Computing	D Cunliffe, G Elliott	978-1904995-05-0
User Interface Design	J Le Peuple, R Scane	978-1-903337-19-6
Visual Programming	D Leigh	978-1-903337-11-0
Access 2002: An Advanced Course for Students	S Coles, J Rowley	978-1904995-06-7
Access 2000: An Introductory Course for Students	S Coles, J Rowley	978-1-903300-14-5
Access 2000: An Advanced Course for Students	S Coles, J Rowley	978-1-903300-15-2
Excel 2002: An Advanced Course for Students	J Muir	978-1-84445-005-3
Excel 2000: An Introductory Course for Students	J Muir	978-1-903300-16-9
Excel 2000: An Advanced Course for Students	J Muir	978-1-903300-17-6
Word 2000: An Introductory Course for Students	S Coles, J Rowley	978-1-903300-18-3
Word 2000: An Advanced Course for Students	S Coles, J Rowley	978-1-903300-19-0
The Small Book of Big Presentation Skills	R. K. Bali, A. Dwivedi	978-1-904995-17-3
Key Skills Level 1: Information and Communication Technology	R Whitley Willis, M Kench	978-1-904995-27-2
Key Skills Level 2: Information and Communication Technology	R Whitley Willis, M Kench	978-1-904995-26-5
Key Skills Level 1: Communication; Application of Number; Information and Communication Technology	R Whitley Willis, L Gabrielle	978-1904995-10-1
Key Skills Level 2: Communication; Application of Number; Information and Communication Technology	R Whitley Willis, L Gabrielle	978-1904995-17-9

To order, please call our order hotline on 01202 712909 or visit our website at **www.lexden-publishing.co.uk** for further information.

Printed in the United Kingdom
by Lightning Source UK Ltd.
122627UK00001B/3-52/A